Introduction

Hello reader I am Stephen Rowlands, I have been involved
am a spiritual trance healer and medium, mental medium,
demonstrating mediumship in spiritualist churches since 198., . also teach general
spiritual development in spiritual development circles, I also love to write poetry, so I
intend this book to be a brief biography of myself, sharing excerpts of my life and
realisations with you and also my poetry, I hope you enjoy reading.

Stephen Rowlands

Opening The Door

I have been asked many times, how I got into spiritualism, in fact I wish I had a
pound, for every time I have told the tale, of how I got into spiritualism so here goes. I
have always been able to sense and feel things, for as long as I can remember,
mainly other people's emotions. Or having images within my mind, showing me
what was to come in the immediate future, my first memory of this I was 4 years old,
we were living in Datchet, in a lovely Victorian house it was Boxing Day that year.
Myself and my cousin Brian were watching television, Jack and the Beanstalk if I
remember correctly, well it was 1964. I had this very strong image in my mind of my
bed being on fire, I told Brian my bed was on fire, he said do not be silly it is my
cigarette, I played up so much my Dad went to investigate. Beside my bed was a 2
bar electric heater it was turned on, close to the blankets on my bed the blankets
were smouldering, my Dad switched off the fire and put out the blankets.

Although I rarely see spirit and if I do it is usually just from the shoulders up, or a quick
flash of a full physical form, which I see out of the corner of my eye, I have always
been able to sense spirit standing close to me, communicating with me in emotion,
can you imagine how it feels to a boy, who does not understand what is happening
to him. I can tell you it is very unnerving, and at times frightening. The first life event
that had a real impact on me, was the passing to spirit of my grandfather I was 7
years old. I could not believe that my granddad had died, because even at that
young age I believed that life was eternal, my granddads physical death came as a
total shock to me.

We used to have legendary bonfires for Guy Fawkes night, over The Gulley that year
1967, and I really feared my granddad would appear in giant form for all to see, that
image was very powerful within my mind. November 5th came granddad did not
appear in giant form.

I was relieved but questioning why did he not show himself, when I feel him so close
to me he is still alive, this emotion has perplexed me all my life, and I have now
made this emotion public, to which I am glad that I am finally sharing it.

Can you imagine how it feels to a child, to have their mind and senses bombarded like this, there are many people like me throughout the world like me, I reach out to you all, please seek guidance and spiritual development. I went on like this for a number of years, becoming more shy and introverted.

I left school and after 18 months in the army, I started work at Hire Service Shops. I was the yardman, my job to keep the yard clean and tidy load and unload lorries, through this job I met Brain North, he was the electrician there fixing and servicing electrical tools for hire, his nickname was Gnu from the famous teabag advert at the time, because he was always drinking tea, he was also vice president of Slough Spiritualist Church.

The store manager was also a Spiritualist, I would have lengthy conversations with Brian, I would discuss with him what had been happening to me. He gave me the answers to my questions. I will be eternally thankful for Brian North, because he gave me answers to questions. and all of a sudden I did not feel quite so weird, the other lads I worked with warned me off Brian, saying he was a nutter and trying to convert me into a cult. I know now this was more fear than knowledge that made them warn me away from Brian.

Eventually Brian invited me to Slough Spiritualist Church to attend a service, I was concerned Brian would set something up for me, although I was compelled to go to Slough Spiritualist Church to investigate, I did not tell Brian when I would visit. New Year's day 1978 I visited Slough Spiritualist Church, I was impressed by the friendliness of the people there, I turned up on my Honda CG 125 wearing a bomber jacket jeans and a white scarf, please forgive me I was 17 what must have they thought, the mediums that night were Mr and Mrs Zealey, Mrs Zealey was a trance medium, I knew it would be religious as Slough was a Christian Spiritualist Church, but overall I was not impressed with the mediumship that night, after the service during tea and biscuits, a little old lady called Ada came to speak with me, she had been resident medium at Slough for over 40 years, she gave me a message from spirit that was so darn accurate, I had to investigate further and decided to attend on a regular basis, that was the beginning of a life long journey.

Spiritual Development

Christian Spiritualism had opened its doors to me, and it was lovely to feel accepted, not strange or different. it was normal to see and sense not weird, I started to go to church, twice a week on a Wednesday and Sunday, as I was embracing this whole new world that was opening up to me. Seeing mediums pass messages to loved ones who were present, seeing the comfort, help, and upliftment, the messages were giving, to the people who were receiving them, I thought to myself I would like to be able to do that.

I had a inner feeling that I could possibly one day, progress into being a platform medium, serving Spirit and giving people upliftment, through the teachings and messages of Spirit. I was seeking something I could excel in, where I could make my parents proud of me, although I was only 18 years old, I had not been much of a success at anything, I left school with a grade 5 CSE English the school only gave me that certificate, so I did not leave school without any qualifications at all, I had no interest in school, and I must also admit to being very lazy. My laziness continued into working life in and out of jobs, and being constantly reminded by parents and family what a failure I was, I was seeking my niche in life where I could excel.

The Seven Principles of Spiritualism:

1. The Fatherhood of God

2. The Brotherhood of Man

3. Communion of Spirits and the Ministry of Angels

4. The Continuous Existence of the Human Soul

5. Personal Responsibility

6. Compensation and Retribution hereafter for all the good and evil deeds done on Earth

7. Eternal Progress open to every Human Soul

Spiritualism was providing me that niche, as I had a growing hunger for knowledge, of all spiritualism could teach me, back in 1978 the teachings of Spirit, were very much taught as a way of life, it was ok to make a mistake as long as you learned from that mistake, I was learning that this earth plane, that we all live on and share, is one big learning ground a school for the soul. I was learning about the levels of spirit.

And that we as souls bring to this earth plane, many different levels of understanding. The reasoning for why we have so much conflict on our earth plane, from disagreements with family and friends to world war, from the liars, cheaters, the greedy for money and power, people who exert there will through violence. To those people who are peaceful, selfless, and loving. And all the levels of understanding between love and hate, it is here on this earth plane, that we come here to learn how to love unconditionally, love is a massive spectrum of emotion, from divine unconditional/universal love, at the top of the spectrum. To hatred greed anger jealousy at the bottom of the spectrum, and that our souls vibrate at varying levels of this spectrum, through our emotions and level of understanding. It was up to us who were aware, and walking a spiritual pathway, to have compassion, for those of a lesser understanding, and at times forgiveness for those of a lower level of understanding, and to live and speak our truth, with love and compassion. To sow the seeds of learning, for those souls of a lower understanding, the teachings of Spirit, are love kindness and compassion tolerance forgiveness, and that we who walk a spiritual pathway, are in service to everyone and everything.The first thing I ever read in Slough Christian Spiritualist Church, was BE HUMBLE IN SERVICE, that one statement has been my guide throughout my spiritual service.

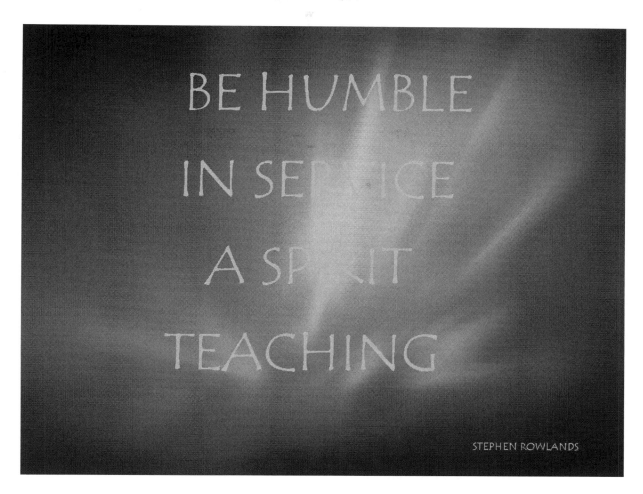

BE HUMBLE
IN SERVICE
A SPIRIT
TEACHING

STEPHEN ROWLANDS

Over the next 3 months, mediums were telling me from the platform, I could develop into being a spiritual healer and medium, although I was seen as to young to become a medium, my Spirit Guides wished to use me as a powerhouse, this meant providing spiritual power, for the spiritual healer and his or her Spirit Guides. A power booster is the best way to describe it, I was invited by Brian North, to join him in the healing sanctuary to be the powerhouse, for him and his healing guides, this was a real step forward for me, and I was very excited about it. I was finally meeting spirit on a level playing field, to be able to embrace spirit, and to find out why they wanted to be around me, and make themselves known to me. The healing sanctuary has a blue light one end of the room, and a red light the other, I had already learned that blue was the main healing colour, I asked Brian why the red and blue lights, he replied it is easier to see spirit in this light, there was a table by the wall in the middle of the room, with religious icons on it and pictures of native American healing guides, and two chairs opposite each other in the middle of the room.

A lady entered the healing sanctuary, and sat down ready to receive healing, Brian asked me to sit in the other chair, and to imagine the lady in the chair with a blue light all around her, and to send my love to her in thought, Brian said a opening prayer invoking inviting spirit to come forward, and channel healing energy through him, the atmosphere within the sanctuary changed, it started to feel a bit warmer, it also felt like other people had entered the healing sanctuary, although I could not see them I could feel them beside me, and moving around the room moving around Brian. there was this growing energy within the sanctuary, a beautiful indescribable feeling of unconditional love, Brian's breathing got a bit deeper and he put his hands over the ladies shoulders, as I shut my eyes I could feel my hands getting warmer and warmer, heat generating from the middle of my palms. this continued for approx. 20-30 minutes, although in that environment you do lose all track and sense of time, Brian then asked the lady if she felt ok she replied that she felt good, and also that she could feel another pair of hands moving over her, and that she felt much better. That was my first experience of giving spiritual healing, and I loved it and wanted to do it more and more. As time went on and the more I sat in the healing sanctuary working as a power house.

For Brian and his healing guides, I was being mentally drawn to where peoples pain and illness was, on a physical level and I would tell people where they were hurting, although diagnosis is very frowned upon today, it was a perfectly normal thing to do back in 1978, and I agree we are not doctors so we shouldn't be giving diagnosis, this was also the start of my third eye and mediumship awareness opening up.

ABSENT HEALING

I was also introduced to and encouraged to do absent healing, the easiest way to describe absent healing is prayer, when we break prayer down it is in actual fact thought, I was being taught that thought is energy and the most powerful thing within the universe, if we infuse our thoughts with love and send those thoughts to people, the energy of our loving thoughts can help them to heal, and asking God and healing guides, to give the healing that was necessary, so I started to give absent healing every Friday night from my bedroom at home, there was a lady at church called Sue, who I had become friendly with she suffered with a bad back, that at times would incapacitate her. I started to send her absent healing as time went by, within my minds eye I could see a bedroom, with a Victorian type bed in it my view was from the head end, and I could see a dressing gown hanging on the rail of the foot end of the bed, also a dressing table with an oval mirror opposite against the wall. After a few months of sending Sue absent healing, she asked me at church did I send my absent healing out on a Friday night, I confirmed to her that I did and that I could see a bedroom, within my mind's eye Sue asked me to describe the bedroom, I did and she said that's my bedroom. I was very astounded and amazed by her comment it was a real shock, but a nice shock if you know what I mean, Sue went on to say she could see my face to her right, as she lay in bed on a Friday night and this was the view I was getting of her bedroom. I did not realise or know that at the time, I was actually astral projecting myself mentally through my healing thoughts, this was a new development for me, and I did not realise that I was really opening up to spirit.

Sat in church one sunny warm Sunday evening, on the platform that evening was the trance medium Berenice Watts. who gave the address and messages in trance, with her spirit guides and loved ones, communicating through her. I was very drawn to Berenice and had a strong feeling a knowing, that spiritually she would teach me, little did I know at that point what a major part, Berenice would play in my spiritual development.

I was invited into Marjorie and Don Jacksons spiritual development circle, in Iver this excited me as I was being told by mediums, that I could develop mediumship and by others, that I was to young at 19 years old, to develop mediumship and that I was not gifted at all, this was a challenge to me as I really needed to excel in something.

Developing my spiritual awareness is something I really wanted to do, and to prove the doubters wrong. Don and Marjorie's circle was held every Friday night, at their home there was Don, Marjorie, myself Nancy and John we sat in the living room, in a circle Marjorie would do the prayer of invocation, and we would sit quietly hands on laps palms upwards,

In a kind of meditative state freeing our minds, of our material worries woes physical aches and pains, and seeing waiting to see what spirit wished to inspire us with, images within the minds eye, feelings of those spirits that were coming around us in the circle, and any messages they wished to share.

This went on for a good few weeks, although at the end of the evening when it was time to give off what we had received, I had nothing to give as I felt I did not experience anything. I was disheartened by this although Marjorie and Don encouraged me to stick with it, then Marjorie would do the closing prayer and we would have tea and biscuits, we continued to sit over the weeks, and I was being drawn to bend physically, forwards backwards from side to side, my arms outstretched in front of me to the sides and above my head, I felt this was all very strange, but the others did not bat an eyelid, so I carried on allowing this to happen to me, I asked Marjorie about it and she said do not worry, its just spirit adjusting to your physical body.

Zangu Zulu Spirit Guide

So I continued sitting and bending physically, until one night we were sitting in a low light, I looked over at Don and all of a sudden his head disappeared before my eyes, and different heads replaced his a native American, china man, a guy with a bowler hat, people of all different nationalities were appearing, this frightened me but amazed me at the same time, as it was the first time I had ever experienced this. My breathing started to get deeper and deeper, my consciousness was getting very inward until I felt about an inch tall within myself, I could hear my breathing getting deeper and more guttural, I could also feel this energy power however you want to describe it, getting stronger and stronger within me I felt I had no physical control over myself, to be honest I was crapping myself as I had no control, this energy power intelligence I could not describe it at the time, had total control over me, I heard Marjorie say have you come in peace, my head was turned from left to right as to say no, now I was really worried I was looking from within outwards, I did not know what was happening to me, and I had no control Marjorie then said have you come to give healing, my head was moved up and down to say yes. Marjorie asked who have you come to give healing to, my arm was pointed towards John, who's spine was crumbling he wore a big surgical belt, and he had to have gold injections into his spine. Amazingly I was stood up and walked towards John.

As I moved closer to John my hands were pointed towards him, fingers closed and outstretched, my hands started to shake very rapidly, and from within myself I could see yellow, red, blue, green, beams of light shooting out of my fingers and into John. I was shocked amazed and wondering what the hell was happening to me, gradually the power holding me began to decrease, Marjorie asked what is your name, a deep guttural voice in a whisper, came from me my name is Zangu, I was sat down and over a few minutes I began to compose myself, and came back into the room, Marjorie explained that Zangu is a healing guide and was told whilst he was with me, that he had been waiting to work with me since before I was born.

I cannot describe to you how that felt, this was my first experience of trance. The closing prayer was said and we had tea and biscuits.

I continued sitting in Marjorie and Don's development circle, for a few weeks more spirit had started to mentally, give me messages and Zangu would come though me in trance. He was also making his presence felt in the healing sanctuary, as Brian felt I was now advanced enough to channel healing, the power he brought through was amazing, and the temperature would really go up in the healing sanctuary, and people were saying they really felt the benefit of the healing power Zangu brought through, although I was starting to have nightmares.

This concerned my parents and myself as I suffered some pretty horrific nightmares as a child, these nightmares were coming back with a vengeance I assured my parents it was nothing I was doing at the spiritualist church, causing the nightmares to return. I walked into church one evening, and sitting in the foyer was a lovely medium by the name of Mrs Brotherton, Frank the president of the church was arguing with a lady, about me saying I was ungifted and to young to develop, the lady was saying just because I was young it did not mean I was not gifted. Don't mind me I thought Mrs Brotherton sat there quietly smiling. During her demonstration of mediumship she came to me with a message, she was telling me from spirit that they were opening a door for me, and behind that door there was many spiritual gifts,

Waiting for me to develop and use with spirit in spiritual service, and that I had a very long way to go on the spiritual path, and many would come to me to be uplifted by these gifts, After the service Frank invited me into his church circle, I will leave you the reader to make your mind up about that.

I was reluctant to leave Marjorie and Don's circle, but mistakenly felt by joining Franks church circle, it would be a way of progressing, as Frank was giving his circle the hard sell. I was still very much learning and naïve, about the right course for spiritual development. So I joined Franks circle, Marjorie and Don were lovely told me to be guided by spirit, and wished me well on my spiritual path, there is not a lot I can say about Franks circle, because spirit really did not communicate with me in that circle, I heard a woman singing in the kitchen one night, no one physical was in the kitchen, and once I was drawn to lay face down on the floor, arms outstretched to the side feet together, I later found out that this is the universal sign of humility.

My nightmares had gradually got a lot worse, I was waking up with a violent jolt screaming my head off, other times I would be falling from the ceiling in my bedroom, with this demonic face above me chasing me, I would wake up with a violent jolt, and be thrown to the other side of the room screaming, one night I woke up screaming kicking the chest of drawers, the other side of the bedroom. Zangu was also coming through as and when he pleased, this was at times embarrassing and dangerous.

My parents were very worried about me, and started talking about getting me psychiatric help, no one at church could give me an answer to the nightmares, I was having, at the time I was working at Bryce Whites Timber Yard in Langley, loading and unloading lorries. I was sent on a forklift driving course which I passed, to celebrate I went across the road to my local pub The Chestnuts, and got myself very drunk directors bitter, and rum and coke was my tipple at the time, I staggered home and went to sleep.

I was falling from the ceiling again, with demonic face chasing me I woke up with a jolt, wedged between my bed, and an old cabinet type record player, I had inherited from my parents.

And in that second I felt a hand grab the back of my head, and force my head down on the corner of the record player, with such force the corner of the record player went through my chin.

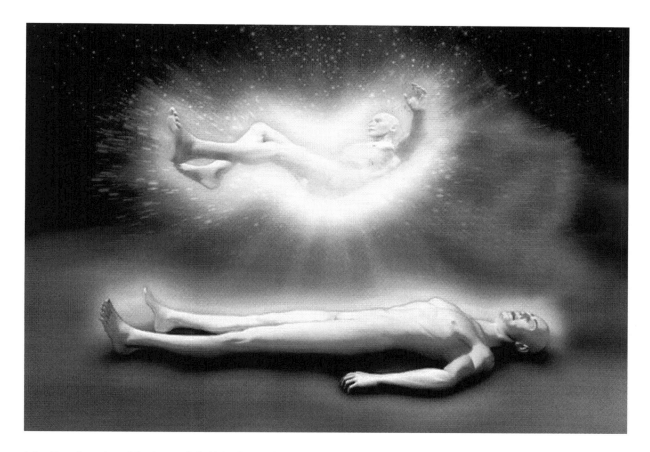

My Dad rushed in I couldn't talk as 3 teeth with gum were under my tongue, I was bleeding heavily, Dad went and got me a tea towel to hold to my mouth to help stop the bleeding, come on Dad said we are going up the hospital, so still drunk wearing my underpants, Dad took me to Wexham Park Hospital. When we arrived in casualty there had been a big fight at one of the local clubs, because of my injury the police thought I was involved in the fight, my Dad said what in his underpants no he has had a nightmare, the look on the policeman's face was classic, I was given emergency surgery, to repair my chin and teeth they could give me an anaesthetic as I was drunk, I saw everything in the stainless steel on the light above my head, I felt everything the surgeon was doing. He wired and stitched the 3 teeth under my tongue back into place, and put 13 stitches in my chin, I remember vividly the big needle for the penicillin injection, when we got home there was 2 teeth sticking out of the record player, yes it hurt like hell the next day I went to the hospital dentist, to have my teeth put into dental clamps for the next 6 months, to hold them all together. The next night I went to Slough Christian Spiritualist Church, looking like frankensteins monster, with 13 stitches in my chin and heavily bruised down the right side of my face, I was a bit shocked as no one said a word, after the service Nancy and Ken approached me, and said do you remember a medium called Berenice Watts, I said yes I did and that I enjoyed her work. Nancy told me that Berenice ran a discussion group in Ruislip, and would I like to go with them as they could see I was in a state, and they felt Berenice could help me. The following Wednesday we went along to Berenice's discussion group.

The average age of the people there was 40 upwards, I was 19 years old so I felt a bit young stupid and shy to say anything, but I listened with interest to the discussion.

Afterwards Nancy and Ken Introduced me to Berenice, Nancy said to her Steve's got some problems can you help him. Berenice took one look at me and, said its going to take more than 5 minutes to sort you out, can you come round for a coffee and chat next week, I agreed as was desperate for help some control over my life, as the nightmares were continuing, and my parents were getting serious about me seeing a psychiatrist, we made arrangement for me to meet her and her husband Ian for a chat.

The following week I went along to Berenice and Ian's, I told them of my experiences and my nightmares, admitted I was drunk when my face got smashed up. And that Zangu was coming through whenever he felt like it, Berenice explained to me that I was very open to spirit, and was very annoyed that I had not been taught how to close down to spirit, she explained to me that it was very important to close down to spirit, as we need to live our material lives, also spirit will use a open channel 24/7, this will have a very detrimental effect on a channel mentally and physically, especially as all and sundry and those from lower levels of spirit, are very drawn to the light of an open channel, and can be very harmful to a channel depending on the state, of the spirits coming close to the channel.

And also alcohol is a depressant but also makes us wide open to spirit, if we are not properly closed down. Her guides told her that I was being used on a astral level for rescue work, to take those on lower levels of spirit into the light and higher levels of spirit, Berenice taught me how to close down, and to do the closing down meditation, before I went to sleep and before I got up in the morning. By asking God and spirit guides for protection, and imagining a blue and green wall around myself, and stating nothing could penetrate it, would give me the protection I needed, Berenice added that my spirit guides were also being very lazy, by not protecting me, Berenice then invited me into her circle to sit for spiritual development.

I was amazed and delighted, that Berenice had invited me into her development circle, it was like jumping from infant school to university, I was very much taught how to close to spirit, also how to open to spirit correctly, how to control my guides and to communicate with them, Berenice is a trance medium so I was taught trance, how to come in and out of trance properly, my guides were taught how to respect and look after me as a physical channel, they wanted to use me so they are responsible for looking after me. other than myself and Berenice there was Ian her husband, and Ron and Pauline a couple also sat in the circle, we would each in turn have to bring a guide through to talk on a set subject.

My favourite was Li an oriental guide, who channelled through Ian his talks were very informative and funny, on how spirit works, universal law, levels of spirit, reincarnation. We were taught how to give an inspired address from our guides, how to give messages from spirit, by cutting out unnecessary bits like names and anniversaries, sand, tarot, playing cards, crystal ball, psychometry, How to channel energy, meditation, one of the more gruelling exercises she would put a picture, in an envelope and we would have to tell her, what or who was in the picture and describe what we saw felt. One night in Berenices circle I arrived, and the bowl of sand was there, she told me I was going to do a sand reading with a difference, after opening the circle Ian channelled the energy of a guide, into the sand I had to tell them who the guide was.

As I looked into the shapes and shadows in the sand, in my minds eye I could see like a monastry with a silver lining around it, I could also see a group of bhuddist monks walking a path to this temple, they were being attacked for the food they had with them, one got hit over the head, instantly in a split second everything went black, and a massive electric like shock through me, then I was back in the room, Ian told me the guide was in actual fact his guide Li, he was a bhuddist monk, and he was murdered for the food he had with him, and is temple was called the temple of silver light.

Sadly Berenice's circle lasted 9 months, as Berenice and Ian moved to Crawley to live, and it was to far for us to travel, I still feel a link to Berenice's circle and my fellow sitters, I will be forever grateful to her for her help and teaching, I also teach the same way as she did very disciplined. I have been working off what I learned in that circle, for the past 37 years it was way ahead of its time, and still is today because it was universal spiritual teaching, as a way of life.

Healing Spirit

As Above So Below

I am not really sure how to tell you this part of my spiritual journey, as it is not a talked about or researched subject, but is worthy of further investigation for our understanding of, the progression of our spirit after physical death, we always say a nasty, wicked, or evil person will go to hell, when they pass over into spirit, and a good person will go to heaven, and be surrounded by angels when they pass over to spirit, there is a lot of truth in this analogy, because our spirit is what we truly are, spirit guides have told me that we create our own heaven or hell in spirit, by our thoughts, emotions, and actions, here on the earth plane. Our spirit is energy a consciousness that survives physical death, there are many levels of consciousness within the world of spirit,that we rise or fall to upon the event of our physical death.

Consciousness can only exist in a level that is vibrating at the same frequency as itself, like attracts like hence why there are many levels of spirit, within the human race there are many different levels of understanding, and this reflects through to the spirit world as above so below. It is spirits that find themselves on a low level of spirit, that need healing to rise towards the light, and ascend to a higher level of spirit, they are at a low level for many reasons, mainly for dark emotions, thoughts, actions, and deeds on the earth plane, whereby they have selfishly put their own needs above others, or they feel they still have things to do here on the earth plane, to right wrongs or to gain forgiveness from someone living in the physical, or they have died suddenly at an accident or by the hand of another, and they still feel the pain and fear of their physical death, or they simply do not know they have physically died especially if sudden death or they had no knowledge or belief in an afterlife, or believe that there is nothing after physical life. We carry our emotions thoughts and deeds over to spirit as above so below, and they stay close to the earth plane vibrating at a dense physical level.

Spirit vibrating at a low level will come to us for help to help them raise their vibration, and to be guided towards the light there are also spirit guides, that work to help low level spirit to ascend to the light, rescue work circles here on the earth plane work alongside spirit guides, and are devoted to helping low level spirit to ascend to the light and higher vibration, and this is where my story begins, back in 1978 when I first started to explore spiritualism, I was sitting for spiritual development and very open to spirit, I had 3 dreams over a period of a few months, each dream was set in a graveyard at night. The first dream I was walking in a graveyard, and had a very strong sense that I must look for and find one particular grave, I did not know which grave but knew I had to find a grave, although in my dream it was night time, there was a light permeating through the darkness turning my surroundings, to a sort of dark blue and grey, I remember thinking in the dream what am I doing here, but I knew I really must find this grave, although I did not know why I must find the grave, eventually I came across this very large grave, with a stone plinth and a sculptured head of a man on it, with like three stone serrated rails over the grave meeting in the middle above the grave, I stood looking at the grave for a while and then the eyes on the head opened. I woke up in the physical screaming and terrified. The second dream was the same graveyard with me having. a very strong urge to find this grave, although with some trepidation as the last dream terrified me, I thought is this a lucid dream, as I know I am back in the same graveyard looking for a grave, that I know there is something evil about it, telling myself to be strong I pressed on, I found the grave the eyes on the head opened, it opened it's mouth and a real deep loud drone come out of it's mouth, everything seemed to vibrate I woke up terrified and screaming, although I was now conscious in my bed at home, I questioned my dream was it a lucid nightmare, could I have changed the dream and dreamt of something much more pleasant.

In the third dream I was joined by a boy and a girl, they were about my age late teens, they told me they were going to help me find the grave, this is very strange I thought why would they want to be here with me in my dream, they asked me what I would do when we found the grave, I said to them I do not know the grave terrifies me, it moves and talks I really do not know why I keep coming back here, we found the grave but it was in a different place, and was very different to how it had appeared before, it was close to the church and it was like a brick box with a gravestone laid on top, and on top of that was the stone head, surrounding the grave was an old black railing pointed with pointed rails, the girl asked me do you know who is buried here. I said I do not know but there must be a reason for me to keep coming back. Here, at that point the stone head turned round to face me. And in a deep man's voice spoke my name, once again I woke up screaming and terrified. The question for me was why I had the three dreams, what was the purpose and reason for me having three dreams about a grave in a graveyard, and who were the young boy and girl, a few months went by and one evening, I was sitting in Berenice Watts development circle, for the meditation she asked us to walk down a Victorian street, I visualized a Victorian street and in my visualisation it was night time, I tried to visualise the Victorian street scene in daylight, but it kept going back to night, so I just stayed with night there were theatres to my left all lit up, and Victorian ladies and gentlemen dressed in there finery, walking up and down the street, it was a fun happy feeling of people out for entertainment and fun, across the road there was a graveyard, I immediately knew it was the graveyard in my three dreams.

Surrounding the graveyard were black pointed railings, there was a large gold building, all lit up with lights shining on it, inset into the outer wall was red square with gold trim, the people walking down the street seemed to be celebrating the fact the gold building was there.

On the pavement outside the gold building stood a Victorian gentleman, with top hat a black beard wearing formal evening dress, he was staring right at me, I felt this is strange why is he staring at me I also felt glued to the spot, but also that me and the Victorian gentleman were all to do with this gold building and feeling of celebration, Berenice called us back into the room to interpret our meditations, I described my meditation to Berenice and told her about my three dreams, and that I strongly felt the gold building was the grave in the 3 dreams, Berenice explained to me that I had been used by spirit to help raise a spirit from the grave, because there are spirits who come into the physical earth vibration, and do not learn and grow whilst attached to the physical body, and lead a very negative life in the physical, when the physical body dies they cannot see a way out and stay attached to the physical body, she felt the Victorian gentleman was the spirit who was helped into the higher light vibration, the atmosphere of celebration was the Victorian gentleman, being welcomed into the higher realms of spirit, the gold building was the symbol of the spirit being raised from the grave. the teenage boy and girl in my dream were spirit helpers, sent to help me raise this spirit, myself in spirit form has a strong living physical earth vibration, and this was of use to spirit to help raise the spirit from the grave. Think of my story what you will, it was all very real for me and at times very frightening, at the time of the three dreams I had not been taught to close down, and was being used by spirit to do rescue work, as was done with the Victorian gentleman, spiritualism and especially Berenice Watts gave me answers to questions, and helped me to understand and control what was happening to me, the one thing I learned from this, apart from spiritual protection is what we do in life, our thoughts emotions and actions echo in eternity as above so below.

First Steps

Wondering how to write about my 37 years of service to spirit, I cannot remember everything in chronological order, but I have many memories, and often find myself relaying those memories to others, by saying I will tell you a story, a story that fits in with the conversation at the time, and hopefully inspires and teaches at the same time, so now with this book I will relay to you some of my memories, and I really hope you enjoy reading my story.

During my time of sitting in development circle and attending Slough Spiritualist Church, there were a few people who would encourage me, on my spiritual pathway as a developing healer and medium, but there were also a few who saw me as a complete upstart, due to my young age and inexperience of life, there was a lot of talk about me some to my face and some behind my back, as to my suitability to become a platform medium.

And unfortunately some would speak unkindly about me to the demonstrating medium that evening, two mediums I remember in particular were Marjorie Nolan and Mrs Weekes, Marjorie Nolan said to me one evening from the platform. That I was not spiritually gifted at all and maybe in 10 year's time, I maybe able to pick up a glimmer of something from spirit, and to stop wasting spirits energy, and that I would never be good enough to work on the platform.

The church was full everyone looking at me as she tore my character and my personality to shreds, with a very smug looking Frank the church president smirking at me, I was 19 years old and I felt totally decimated when I left the church that evening, Mrs Weekes was just plain horrid to me on and off the platform, one time outside of the church, she asked me my star sign, I told her my star sign was Gemini, she then ripped into me telling me all that was negative about being a Gemini, the real dark side of the star sign and she told me that the dark side of Gemini was me.

One evening I walked into church and sitting in the foyer, was the lovely medium Mrs Brotherton, a medium who always demonstrated with a lot of humour, as her spirit guides would always show her pies and sausages floating above peoples heads, Frank the church president was arguing with a lady about me, saying that I would never make a platform medium, the lady arguing in my defence saying how would you know he has a lot of life ahead of him, I did not know what to say so I went into the church and sat down, although I was angry with Frank for talking about me in that way, during the demonstration of mediumship Mrs Brotherton came to me with a message from spirit, telling me I was very gifted and one day a door would open, and all my gifts would be waiting for me, and many people would come to watch and listen to me, and through the gifts of spirit great teaching healing and upliftment would be given through me, I was obviously over the moon with the message, I had received from spirit as it was an endorsement of my spiritual pathway, and service to spirit.

Also wiping the smug smirk off Frank's face was pure gold, although 39 years later I have not reached the state of development that spirit spoke of that night, I live in the knowledge that life is a process of spiritual development, and all will come at the right time if I continue to develop, so I say to all young and old know in your heart that you wish to serve spirit, stay within your truth and go as far as spirit wish to take you, I knew within my own heart that I had found my niche in life, and serving spirit from the platform was something that I was going to do, no amount of criticism was going to deter me from my purpose and pathway.

In 1982 I had not sat for spiritual development for 2 years, my spirit guides were constantly saying to me, "We want to work through you on the platform" this nagging went on and on, until finally I gave up and said to them "OK I GIVE UP YOU WIN, I WILL WORK ON THE PLATFORM, BUT IF I MAKE A FOOL OF MYSELF, ITS ALL YOUR FAULT." And I started writing to local churches, offering myself to serve their churches on the platform. As I had not opened to spirit for a couple of years, except to send out absent healing , or channel healing in the healing sanctuary I needed to establish my link with spirit,

I joined an open development circle, at Slough Spiritualist Church. The circle was run by a guy called Harry and his lady wife, I have never liked open circles as I feel they are dangerous, because people can come and go on a weekly basis, so the energies change, a lot because of this also you don't know what level of spirit people are bringing in with them, but this open circle had a few regular sitters, so it should be ok to sit, and attune my mediumship with spirit again. We sat typically male female next to each other, to balance the energies the idea being, that the male energy would protect the female energy.

If a lower form spirit got into the circle. I was sat next to a young lady named Sue, every week she would bring through in trance, a spirit claiming to be Mary Queen of Scots. But something did not feel right with this spirit, so I went along to Langley Library, and researched the life of Mary Queen of Scots, now armed with the necessary information, I went along to open circle to check this spirit out, but methinks this spirit was one step ahead of me, and was aware of my plans to check her or it out. As we sat I spoke to the spirit, as it was coming through Sue in trance, Sue's head was turned to face me, her eyes were big and jet black her face contorted with anger, the vibration of rage, became stronger and stronger in the room. As this spirit was moving Sue's head to look at other sitters, the spirit seemed to be linking with other sitters, because as soon as she had looked at them, the sitters were overcome by a strong feeling of nausea, a couple of people started vomiting.

My breathing got deeper and deeper, it was my Zulu guide Zangu, starting to come through me in trance, I was very happy for Zangu to come through, and allowed him to do so, as I had no idea of how to get rid of this evil spirit. Through me in trance Zangu, cut the energy lines between the evil spirit and the sitters, people were starting to recover.

Then Zangu turned me towards Sue and the evil spirit, and channelling very powerful energy through me, looking out of myself I could see lots of different coloured, beams of light shooting out of me, reds, yellows, blues, coming from me and into Sue's aura, to expel the evil spirit from her, a couple of minutes later the evil spirit was expelled from Sue, and sent back to wherever it came from. Zangu stepped back from me but my oriental guide Sun Si Sin, stepped into me in trance, and spoke through me to the circle about protection, he reminded the circle to make sure the circle was protected, as well as each sitter should make sure they are protected, as there are low level spirit that are attracted to the light of the circle, and will want to attach themselves to the sitters, as was the case with the so called Mary Queen of Scots.

My oriental guide stood back and I regained my senses, Harry then appeared to go into "trance," and he said virtually what my oriental guide had said, I was a bit put out by this, but hey ho each to their own, I was glad the circle and sitters were safe. I was also perturbed by the lack of understanding, for the need of spiritual protection, as it had been drummed into me at Berenice's circle, I had put my protection in place during the opening prayer, that is why I was unaffected by the low level spirit, which was good really as someone with protection, and strong spirit guides was there to sort the situation out. I only needed this circle to regain my attunement to spirit, so would only stay in it for as long as was necessary.

On another evening in Harry's open circle, he wanted to try out new things with us, so he asked each of us to bring in a personal item, so we could do psychometry on each others items, and give readings from the items, for those who do not know what psychometry is, everything is energy and energy has its own vibrational frequency, so everything we wear or touch, we imprint our own vibrational frequency on it. those who are sensitive and can read and understand vibration, are very good at psychometry, you could give someone a reading off their socks if necessary, simply because the wearer had imprinted their vibration onto the socks, I do get some funny looks when I say that but it is true. I had already done some psychometry in Berenice's circle, so was happy to do psychometry again, as it would help with my attunement, as being able to read vibration as a medium is very important. As spirit do communicate a lot with emotion, and yes our emotions have their own vibrational frequency, to as I said everything is energy.

I was handed a silver pocket watch by Hannah one of the sitters, as I held the pocket watch in my hand, within my minds eye I could see an old man digging up cabbages, I felt strongly the old man was Hannah's Grandfather, and that he had trouble with his knees in life, I relayed this information to Hannah.

And she confirmed the watch belonged to her Grandfather, and that he had an allotment, and one of her memories of him, was of him digging up cabbages on his allotment. I was pleased I was able to pick this information up, and connect Hannah with her Grandfather, I passed the pocket watch back to her, and she gasped I said what's a matter, she said this watch has not worked for years but now its working, and sure enough the pocket watch was ticking away, I cannot say why the watch started working, after years of not working, but it confirms to me Hannah's Grandfather was with her.

I left Harry's circle a few weeks later, as I felt it had served its purpose, my attunement to spirit had been regained on a mediumnistic level, on 5th January 1983 I did my first ever solo platform, at Slough Spiritualist Church, this was a big test for me and spirit, for me to prove to myself and others, that I am a platform medium, and for spirit to back there mouth up and work through me on platform, as they had been nagging me to do, for the previous 2 years the night was a success, and I was now assured that spirit truly wanted to work through me on platform, doing public demonstrations of mediumship

I was approached by Ann Pert a stalwart of Slough Spiritualist Church, and medium of 40 plus years, a sweet but very strong lady who was in her mid 1980's to demonstrate mediumship for her spiritualist group at the old Slough library, I was very honoured to be asked by Ann to serve her group, as she was a knowledgeable and respected medium, as I was in between jobs at the time, I agreed to serve spirit at her group on a Wednesday afternoon, the Wednesday afternoon came along the meeting was held in a large room on the second floor of the library.

I walked in and there was Ann with around 30 pensioners sitting in a circle, Ann then dropped the bombshell, that she expected everyone to get a message from spirit. I told her I did not think I would be able to give everyone a message, but would certainly give it a try, after the opening prayer I commenced to give messages from spirit, the energy was very strong that day, and we managed to give everyone a short message from spirit, although afterwards I was very tired and mentally drained, there was one old gentleman who has remained in my memory since that day, alas I cannot remember his name but during his message, spirit were talking to him about his automatic writing, for those who do not know what automatic writing is, it is where spirit guide the hand of the channel, to write the words they wish to communicate, afterwards he struck up a conversation with me about his automatic writing, as I remember a very interesting conversation, as he had been automatic writing for years, he visited me at my home a couple of times to show me his automatic writing, he had thousands of pages of writing containing teaching and messages from spirit, if only it could have been made into a book, it could have helped so many understand the workings of spirit life and the universe, a lovely man and a true servant of spirit, I will always remember him. I began writing to churches to see if they would book me to serve them as a platform medium, back in the day before email and facebook that's how we did it, to get cancellation work last minute bookings when the serving medium, could not demonstrate that evening.

One of the first churches that got back to me was Maidenhead Spiritualist Church, as the medium had cancelled for that evening, she told me that she had tried ten other mediums, but they were unavailable so we thought we would try you. At the time I used to walk right in front of the person to give them their message from spirit, this led to a few complaints as people in the congregation, liked to see and hear the medium from the front not twisting their necks around to see the medium, I replied that's how I work, I was told they were happy with the work done that evening, but if I wished to serve their church again, I had to learn to speak from the front of the church, so from that day on with my guides we learned to give messages from the front of the church, although the energy seemed weaker from the front, but it gradually grew stronger and it was a very valuable lesson for me to learn.

I learned in Berenice's circle to take my shoes off when working with spirit, for earth power, as spirit are a form of energy, that we have not learned how to record and measure as yet, but it was best to be earthed for safety reasons, as you have an earth on an electric plug. And to draw natural power from the earth, so I went around the church platforms, demonstrating mediumship not wearing my shoes, I became known as the medium who takes his shoes off, one night at Hayes Spiritualist Church, I kept my shoes on as the church had been flooded, and the floor was still wet, I was concerned I might get a bit of trench foot, but was also concerned blocking earth power may affect my link with spirit, but my need to protect my feet won.

I went onto the platform and demonstrated mediumship, the demonstration went well, and after the demonstration a guy sitting in a wheelchair with no legs approached me. He said to me "my guides are telling me you should keep your shoes off when on the platform" he had never seen me demonstrate before, and had no knowledge of me not wearing my shoes whilst demonstrating, WOW I thought what a way to teach me, spirit send me a man with no legs to tell me to keep my shoes off, I will never ever forget how spirit got the message to me, that night and often use that memory, to teach students how spirit work.

I met a lot of lovely people at Hayes Spiritualist Church, and I have fond memories of them all, particularly Bert, and Rocky, Margaret Hanks, Anne Walker, Annie, Ida Escott, Derek Thurlbeck, and Mark Deville. I remember one night giving Derek Thurlbeck a message from platform, his Egyptian guide was telling him via me, he was going to move away from mediumship and teach spiritual philosophy, the world had enough mediums it needed more teachers. Derek was very put out about this message, and he approached me angrily after the service he said to me, " I am going to be a medium, I am meant to be a medium not a philosopher, you got that all wrong." I replied "we shall see" 10 years later I was at a church somewhere, and a person said to me "do you know Derek Thurlbeck" I replied yes I know him the person, told me Derek had now given up his mediumship, and was teaching philosophy, well blow me down I replied, I told Derek 10 years ago he would be doing philosophy, and he did not believe me, teaching me we should never doubt what spirit tell us, because they can see the bigger picture a lot more than we can. One of the platform mediums of the day who I really admired, and looked up to was Derek Markwell, very energetic, funny, and a great communicator for spirit, I suppose I actually took on some of his style when demonstrating, because the way he would communicate the address and spirit messages, in a down to earth way would really touch people on a heart level.

Raising the energy and vibration making spirit communication so much easier, for spirit and Derek as the channel, rather than some of the more flowery monotone mediums of the day, his services were very uplifting for all those who attended. I was serving Ashford Spiritualist Church one summers evening in 1986, it was a Sunday service, I was met by Sheila a lady who I knew from Bracknell Spiritualist Church, she informed me that Derek Markwell who was now sadly suffering from MS and his lady wife were to be present for the service, can you imagine my delight and terror knowing one of my platform heroes, would actually be sitting in the congregation watching me demonstrate mediumship, and the thought of Derek being in the congregation quite honestly terrified me, it was like all my spiritual development and myself were under the microscope, as Derek Markwell was a medium who I truly respected, as I stepped up to the platform I took my jacket off to hang over the chair, swung my jacket round from my shoulder and knocked a vase of flowers flying.

Smashing the vase and flowers on the floor, "Oh Shame Where Is Thy Blush" I really wanted the ground to open up and swallow me. I could not apologise enough, the congregation erupted in laughter and I was hoping the destroyed flowers were not a bad omen for the service. From experience myself and my spirit guides settled quickly to regain our link, as it is the quality of the communication that is paramount, not the mediums embarrassment, it came the time to give the inspired address, I looked at Derek and he looked back at me with so much support in his eyes it was very humbling for me I looked at my guides and said to them "Lets Do It" and we carried on after the service, Sheila came to me and said to me "Derek wants to speak with you" OMG I thought he is going to tell me I'm crap, and that I was under developed to be a platform medium, as he struggled to walk towards me on his walking sticks, I said to Derek "its ok Derek I will come to you" he replied Its ok son I will come to you, he walked up to me looked me straight in the eye and said, "you carry on son great service you carry on" I was absolutely relieved he did not tell me off, and it was so amazing to be encouraged by one of my peers, I told him he was one of my heroes and that I had always admired his work, he said don't be daft son we do what we do for spirit, I will always treasure this memory.

Knowing

My heart open and aware hears the voices of spirit

Voices speaking of love and reassurance

To beloved ones on earth in grief and sorrow

It is my calling to be a voice for the beloved in spirit

To tell the truth of eternal life and death will not us part

My vocation to be a connection of love for spirit

To speak to the beloved ones they left behind

To heal the pain of Death's parting

In life and eternity

Stephen Rowlands

Spiritual Healing

Spirit are always reminding me that I am in actual fact a healer, in this book I will talk of some of the times, that I have been used as a channel for healing, and had the most impact on me as a healer. Although this book should not be taken as documentary proof of spiritual healing, or my gift as a healer none of it can be proven, but it is all part of my life experience as a channel for spirit.

In 1983 I was on a high because I was finally expressing myself truly, being a channel for spirit and I had started serving spiritualist churches, as a medium but I still wanted to continue working as a channel for spiritual healing, I put an advert in the Slough Observer advertising myself as a medium and healer.

In answer to my advert an elderly lady telephoned me, who lived just down the road from me in the alms houses, she told me that due to a medical condition her right knee was very swollen and painful, she asked me if spiritual healing could help, I advised her that as a spiritual healer I could not promise her a cure, but I knew spiritual healing could help her on one level or another, greater inner peace or just to help ease the pain for a while, the lady visited me for spiritual healing the following Saturday, her right knee was very swollen I made her comfortable in an armchair, and asked her to just relax myself and my healing guides would do the rest, I attuned myself to me healing guides, and channelled healing energy to the ladies swollen knee, after 10 - 15 minutes my healing guides stood back to my and the ladies surprise, the swelling on the ladies knee had significantly gone down, and was not painful anymore the lady was very surprised and happy that the spiritual healing had worked, as I was showing the lady out my nan invited her to stay for a cup of tea, the lady was then happily telling my nan about the spiritual healing she had just received, and that it had worked.

I had another phone call from an Asian man telling me his mother was very sick with cancer, in Windsor hospital how much would it cost to make her better, I told him that I did not charge a fee for healing, and I could never promise a cure, he was not impressed with my statement, and asked me why I could not heal his mother for money, I explained that I could never promise a cure as each receives according to their needs, for their spiritual progression in universal life, also that I could never take money from sick people, I told him that I knew spiritual healing can bring relief from pain and help to bring peace to the sick, I would do my best to channel the healing to cure his mother, but there was no way I could guarantee a cure, the man seemed to accept that I could not guarantee a cure, and I agreed to go with him to Windsor hospital, I to channel healing energy to his mother. He picked me up at my home on the agreed day and time, we arrived at the hospital, he said I will stay in the car you go to my mother, and he gave me the ward and bed number his mother was in.

As I approached his mother's bed I could see a frail elderly Asian lady, who looked emaciated by her cancer, it dawned on me that her cancer was terminal, I was quite nervous as at the time spiritual healers in hospitals was frowned upon, a nurse looked at me quite oddly as a young white male, visiting an elderly terminally ill Asian lady,

I introduced myself to the lady she said to me "I give you money make me better" and from her bedside cabinet she pulled out a thick roll of £20 notes, I told her I did not want her money, and that I could not promise to cure her, she kept trying to give me the money, I told her money will not cure her, and healing would help her to be at peace and ease her pain, I managed to calm her down and the lady became still, I outstretched my hands to her, asked healing guides to come close and channel healing through me to the lady, I was concerned I might be thrown out of the hospital for giving spiritual healing, about halfway through the healing, a nurse came and put a screen around us the healing was very powerful for the lady, after about 30 minutes my healing guides drew back, and the healing was complete, I left the lady sleeping and I went to meet her son in the car park.

On meeting her son I told him I could accept the money his mother tried to give me, he became angry and started shouting at me calling me names, as he drove me home, he calmed down a bit and asked me if his mother was going to live, I told him that his mother's condition was way beyond money, and that it was now between her and God, and that I feared she would probably die, and that her death would be a release for her, from her pain and physical body into universal life in spirit, he began shouting at me as he dropped me off at home, calling me a charlatan he tried to give me £20 for my time, I would not accept it reminding him I cannot take money for channelling healing, he drove away shouting and being abusive towards me, this incident left a nasty sickly feeling within me, for a very long time how could they think money, could make their terminally ill mother better, I know people often go to spiritual healers as a last resort, and expect miracles to happen, it is in my teaching that each receives according to their soul needs, at times we are meant to experience suffering in physical life, for the growth of the eternal soul, it is also a simple truth that money cannot buy health, so please whatever your condition please visit a spiritual healer, when you are first diagnosed with a serious illness, I know at the very least it will bring pain relief and peace to you, and help you with the growth of your eternal soul.

Sarah

I have not sought permission from the people concerned, to publish the following account of healing, as I have had no contact with them since 1986, to protect their identity, I will change their names for the purposes of this account.

Way back in 1984 I was at home with my parents, it was a Friday so it was our weekly fish and chip night, as we were waiting for my dad to return from the chip shop, my mum told me of her friend at work, who has a granddaughter who was suffering with stomach cancer, her granddaughter Sarah was 3 years old, Zangu my Zulu guide told me the cancer was in her stomach, but had progressed to her lungs, I told my mum what Zangu had said and my mother replied how did you know" I told my mum that my Zulu guide had told me, my mother went on that Sarah's grandmother Anne, had tried to get Sarah an appointment with spiritual healer Ted Fricker, a respected and well known healer at the time, but had only managed to get Sarah's name on Ted Frickers healing list,

I told my mother that Ted's healing list very probably had thousands of people on it, and the healing Sarah would actually get would be limited.Zangu kept saying to me that we should give Sarah healing, I gulped and offered our healing services to mum for Sarah, to my surprise my mother said that she would talk to Anne at work Monday morning and see what she said, Monday evening my mum told me that she had spoken to Anne, and that Anne would speak to Sarah's parents, and sent thanks for the offer of spiritual healing for Sarah, 3 or 4 days later Anne phoned my mum telling her, that Sarah's parents would try anything to help their daughter, but they wished to meet me first to make sure I was not a weirdo, the following week myself and mum and dad went to meet Sarah's parents and grandparents at Sarah's home.

I was nervous about the meeting but it was Zangu's conviction, that him channelling healing energy through me could help Sarah, that encouraged me to go through with it, it was a positive meeting I explained how Zangu would channel healing through me, and the family gave me and Zangu permission to channel healing to Sarah, on the proviso that Sarah's dad Dave was present in the room, which was no problem at all, the following week we met to channel healing to Sarah, Dave showed me up to Sarah's room she was lying fast asleep in her cot, Dave sat down beside the cot and I called on Zangu to step forward for Sarah's healing, the healing was powerful I could see healing colours shooting from my fingers, and into Sarah's stomach and chest, the healing lasted for around 20 minutes, when downstairs Dave told me he could feel spirit joining us in the room, and he could see the healing colours shooting out from me and into Sarah.

Dave telling me what he experienced during the healing was amazing, as he had no experience of spiritualism or spirit before, and this very much encouraged me as to the strength of the healing being given, and to continue with Sarah's healing, Sarah's parents asked me to visit once a week to channel healing to Sarah, I agreed and my parents agreed to bring me to Sarah's home once a week, this went on for several weeks, Anne told my mother that the doctors could not work out, why Sarah was not losing her hair as she was receiving chemotherapy.

I told my mother that Sarah not losing her hair, was due to the strength of the healing being given, on one particular visit to Sarah's home her grandfather Albert, asked if there was anything they could do to help, whilst me and Dave were upstairs with Sarah, so I got my parents Sarah's grandparents and mum sitting in a circle, and taught them how to send absent healing to Sarah, this was a great idea as it would really boost the healing being given to Sarah, and would help them make a valuable contribution to Sarah's healing, we continued to visit to give healing until Sarah was diagnosed, as being in remission from cancer, and I continued to send Sarah absent healing from home, a couple of years later Sarah was diagnosed as being all clear from cancer, and Sarah's family sent us their thanks and gratitude for our part in Sarah's recovery from cancer, a few years ago my mum told me that Sarah was working as a consultant in a NHS hospital, and that Anne once again sent her thanks, to this day I am so glad to have been a part of Sarah's healing from cancer, helping her to grow into the amazing woman that she is, also I thank Zangu for nagging me and believing in me as his channel, as I lacked the confidence to put myself forward for Sarah, I am also thankful with the greatest gratitude to Zangu and healing guides for Sarah's healing.

Reaching Out

Back in the year 1985 I was preparing to do a demonstration, at Guildford Spiritualist Church, it was a Sunday service so an inspired address, from my spirit guides was a part of the service, my guides had not given me any idea, on what they would like to inspire me to say, but we usually waited until an inspirational paragraph, from a book or a passage from the Bible had been read, then my guides would let me know what to say from the reading, as the reading would become the subject of the address, the vice president of the church at the time, a lady called Vanda sat opposite me, with a book on her lap entitled reaching out, on seeing this my guide a mandarin drew in close to me, inspiring me with the words to say do we not all reach out for something.

We all reach out for the love of another, we all reach out to be understood by others, we all reach out for kindness compassion and strength from others, we all reach out to others to help us to be successful in life, but few reach within to the spirit, where love, understanding strength, kindness, compassion, our drive for success are in abundance, we always look outwards for what we need in life, and it is the cause of a lot emotional pain, when we have the expectation for our emotional and material needs to be fulfilled from external sources, when everything we need for a wholesome life, in a material world are within.

It is a simple truth that all the answers we need are within us, many scoff at this simple truth, and prefer to seek answers from outside of themselves, all we get from that is another person's experience, other than our own that maybe right or wrong for us, and can lead to further personal disasters and torment, looking within to seek the answers we need, means we are connecting with our own truth, and once the answers are found, we can action them and live by our own truth, but first we must put aside all external influences in life, breathe and be silently listening out for the inner voice, that tells us how we truly feel and the best way forward for us in life, the world and the universe is governed by freewill, it is the freewill of everything that effects everything in our lives.

Many feel useless to have any control over their lives, because they feel the freewill of everything controls them, and they could not be more wrong because it is us that dictates our life from within, to surrender the power of our own personal truth is a great betrayal of ourselves, to the control of everything, we are living life the way everything wants us to be, we must connect to the spirit within, seek out our own personal truth and live by it, and not be afraid of how others will perceive us, as long as the way we live life does no harm to others, why cannot we live by our own truth, as spirit we are love, kindness, tolerance, compassion, that is the beauty of who we truly are, so we must reach out with love, kindness, tolerance, and compassion, for ourselves and all others, this is the way and truth of spirit.

What Being A Spiritualist Means To Me

There are a lot of people these days protesting, that spiritualism is not a religion, spiritualism in the UK had to become a religion, so that practitioners such as mediums and healers were not prosecuted, under the out dated witchcraft Act 1735, and to gain charitable status medium Helen Duncan was convicted under the witchcraft act, in September 1944 for claiming to conjure spirits, whilst I agree that spirit never speak of religion as there is no religion in spirit, and spirit do not speak of a god, they speak of divine light, no one can deny who has studied and communicated with spirit, the existence of a universal life and law, that spirit communicate to us here on earth as above so below.

The driving force of universal life is love, and it is love that spirit communicate to us here on earth, and the teachers that mankind built religion around all taught love, many who come into spiritualism in the UK, have come from a Christian background, and the cross in a spiritualist church gives resonance and focus to those from a religious background, who wish to learn more through spirit communication, how things work in the life hereafter and how to progress spiritually, and so enhancing their humanity, spirit guides teach that a church is a building a medium for them to communicate there truths, a group of likeminded people meeting in a building, to commune the teachings of spirit is by definition a religion.

It depends on the energy of love and attunement to spirit within the building, that we and spirit can create together, the creation of love with spirit, depends on the level of attunement of the people within the building, hymns and prayers help us to gain greater attunement to spirit, taking us out of our material physical minds, to higher levels of attunement to spirit, yes all of this is religious ritual, but what is prayer but emotion and thought, spirit communicate to us in emotion and thought, and it is our attunement to love, that spirit need to communicate with us successfully.

Spiritualism has been crusading to prove the existence of eternal life, through spirit communication the facts of the communication proving eternal life, there is far greater communication with spirit, in the teachings spirit pass on to us, the teachings are of universal life and law, for we are spirit living learning and growing in a physical material world, to be a spiritualist is to live and walk with spirit on our earth plane, practising the teachings of spirit, and to be the true messengers of spirit, we must practice love, kindness, compassion, and forgiveness, in our thoughts words and deeds in service to spirit, there is a lot more to mediumship than giving messages, this is what being a spiritualist means to me.

My Grieving For Dad Helping Me To Become A More Compassionate Medium

For many years I could never understand why people, would be so sad for the loss of their loved ones in spirit, their grieving causing them so much emotional pain, and sadness years after their beloved ones, had passed over the veil into spirit. The people I speak of are spiritualists, I stood beneath the spiritualist banner there is no death, and I wrongly felt that the knowledge of the truth there is no death, would be comforting enough for the pain and sadness of grieving, to cease but because I had not suffered the loss of a loved one, I did not understand the emotional kaleidoscope of grieving, even when people were getting messages via a medium, from their loved ones in spirit the pain and sadness still remained with them.

Whilst in spiritual development circle, an oriental spirit guide known to us as Li, came through his channel Ian Watts in trance, as he often did to give us some teaching of universal life in spirit. In his talk he was saying that we should not mourn our loved ones in spirit, as it is only the physical loss of our loved ones that we grieve for, and this to him grieving for our loved ones was selfish of us to do, he accepted that when we first lose a loved one there should be a period of mourning for the physical loss of the loved one, he went on to say that our loved ones are now in a realm of light, and are living within the divine energy of universal and unconditional love. We should be happy for them and allow them to continue, there journey in spirit as they are truly now spirit, and we should love them as spirit beings, and not selfishly mourn their physical loss, over a long period of time.

I held onto Li's teaching for years believing it was selfish to grieve, for the physical loss of our loved ones, although I never spoke of this teaching as I believed, it would cause more hurt to those who had lost loved ones, it is my role as a medium to bring upliftment to others through spiritual teachings, but looking at Li's teaching from a spirit perspective, his teaching is correct and I believe that this teaching, should be given totally from a spirit perspective, to those who are emotionally ready to receive it. As I have often thought we never see things from spirits side of life, and how it effects them in their interactions with us on earth, and in doing so this makes us the selfish ones.

Sadly my Dad passed over the veil into spirit 14/10/15, although his passing was expected as he was very ill, I stood by his bedside with my mother at Wexham Park Hospital, the doctor had just pronounced him physically dead, I held his hand and his voice loudly spoke to me in my head in his voice, "LOOK AFTER YOUR MOTHER" which was totally my Dad as he worships the ground my Mum walks on, my brother arrived and we said our farewells to my Dad, we went back to my mothers I was stunned it was as if time had stood still, but life was going on as everybody and everything was going about their daily business, I raised a glass of whiskey and ice Dads favourite drink to say cheers thanks for everything to him, Dads funeral was arranged for 03/11/15, to give friends from overseas a chance to assemble for his funeral, I took Mum to see Dad in the funeral home.

As I stood over Dad in his coffin there was the real sickening energy of physical death, permeating deep into my gut, a feeling that stayed with me for a very long time, my mother said it is so cold in here Elwyn doesn't like the cold, as she touched his cheek I said Mum he is not here this is just his shell, I took my mother home and prepared Dads Eulogy, as I was nominated to give it, as I was used to talking in front of people, my family sees that I have my uses.

SIGNS

The week after my fathers passing to spirit, I had three demonstrations of mediumship to do, I debated with myself whether I should do them or not, as I was an emotional and mental wreck functioning only to be strong for family, and cope with the rigours of my job, I made the decision to cancel my platform bookings, I knew the churches would understand. Queen was my dads favourite band, I got into the shuttle bus to go pick up staff, I switched on the radio The Show Must Go On by Queen, came blasting out of the radio this could only have been my Dad, as he was a very selfless man, and wanted his children to live life to the full, you may scoff but I know this is the truth.

I have often thought that the belief that our loved ones in spirit, leave a penny when they are near to be a fairytale, a few weeks after my Dads passing to spirit, I called out to my Dad, come on Dad if you are near give me a sign. I proceeded to hoover my flat, I had hoovered every square inch of my flat, as I was putting the hoover away, I looked down and there was a shiny penny looking up at me from the floor. How could I have missed that my flat is tiny, I couldn't have missed it, no its just a fairytale, in the morning I walked down the bottom of the stairs, opened the door to go to work, and there was a shiny penny looking up at me from the paving slab, now I believe spirit leaving pennies as signs to be true.

REALISATION

My dad makes his presence felt most days I speak to him every morning, but I still miss him wish he was still here to talk to and share a joke with, and yes Li that makes me selfish, I live in the physical world where we need our loved ones near, we need their physical presence, as much as it is wonderful to receive a message from our loved ones in spirit, nothing can take away our need to have them physically with us. As a medium I have given the messages and watched the tears flow, there is nothing I can do to dry those tears, the spiritualist message of there is no death, has failed, but with compassion and spiritual teaching we can comfort and uplift.

Reflections

Mortal life is but a glimpse of all things

In our waking consciousness

What are memories

Reflections naught but time can advocate

Time is a useless measure

As our reflections prove

Nothing loses it's forward momentum

In this revolving universe as life goes on

Reflections of love when time makes no sense

Moving forward I cannot go back

To thank you to tell you I love you

I converse with you within this moment

Sadly this moment will leave me

And the future is a time we do not dwell

I turn this moment to the past to be with you

Like an old favourite film I press replay

Sadness manifests as I stumble into the next moment

Seeing your smile feeling your words calling within my heart

Do your best beautiful boy live the best life you can

I tell you with all my heart I promise you the best I can

Knowing you walk with me where time does not exist

And love is eternal and still

Stephen Rowlands

Dedicated to Elwyn Rowlands 27/11/29 - 15/10/15

Guided By Spirit To Cirencester

At home from work in bed tired and weary after a night shift, 07/01/14 I was just dropping off to sleep, when my mobile phone rang "who the hell can that be" I thought, I answered the phone very drowsy and not in a good mood the caller a lady, introduced herself as the booking secretary for Cirencester Spiritualist Church, she told me that they had a cancellation for their divine service Saturday night, and she had found a piece of paper in her mediums book with my name and number on it, but she did not know who had given her my name and number, and how the piece of paper had got into her mediums book, the mediums she had phoned were all busy, so in desperation she thought she might give me a try.

I explained to the lady that although I would love to serve her church, Slough is a long way from Cirencester, would the church be able to meet my fuel expenses, myself and the lady agreed expenses at £30.00, the lady was very baffled as to how she had got my name and number, my only explanation was that I had served Stroud Spiritualist Church back in the 90's, and perhaps someone from there had took my name and number to recommend me, and somehow it had found its way into her mediums book, she told me that is not possible, I confirmed with her that I would serve Cirencester Spiritualist Church at 7.30 pm 11/01/14, we said our goodbyes and as I laid down to sleep, I thought this is a mystery but this service must be meant to be, and spirit must want me to serve there for some reason.

On 11/01/14 I made my way to Cirencester Spiritualist Church nervous and excited, about what my purpose could be for serving spirit there, it was a cold misty winters night I arrived with 45 minutes to spare, before the service began I was greeted with a warm welcome, as I introduced myself as the medium for the evening, it was a medium sized SNU Church, but looking around I felt it was a strict SNU Church this made me a bit nervous, as I had not demonstrated at this level for some time, as I am quite laid back and down to earth in my presentation of philosophy and spirit messages, I was also wearing blue jeans and a navy blue collarless shirt and white trainers, which made me feel quite scruffy and felt strongly from my spirit guides, that I should really smarten up to serve them in Spiritualist Churches, the booking secretary arrived and introduced herself, as we shook hands she said " I really don't know how I got your name and number" I replied " it's a mystery but lovely to be here" I was shown to a side room to meditate and gain attunement to spirit, my spirit guides gathered around me I asked them what is my purpose for being here, Red Cloud just smiled at me thanks I thought, I was very nervous but my spirit guides were coming around me, with such strength I thought just go for it.

SPIRITUALISTS' NATIONAL UNION

LIGHT

NATURE

TRUTH

®

AFFILIATED BODY

The Seven Principles of Spiritualism

The Fatherhood of God.

The Brotherhood of Man.

The Communion of Spirits and the Ministry of Angels.

The Continuous Existence of the Human Soul.

Personal Responsibility.

Compensation and Retribution Hereafter for all the Good and Evil Deeds done on Earth.

Eternal Progress Open to every Human Soul.

The booking secretary popped her head around the door and said it is time, she led me to the platform the church was well attended, which was a refreshing sight as less people attend divine services, as compared to evenings of clairvoyance I took my seat on the platform, nervous and calling on my spirit guides to come closer, as I shut my eyes I could see my grandad and he said to me we are in the moment, I opened my eyes and felt a very strong emotion, as if it was my first time serving spirit at a divine service, I was truly within the moment with spirit, I cannot explain the emotion but it felt euphoric, I was very drawn to the 7 principles of spiritualism hanging on the wall to my left, and I realised that my whole life I had been living not always correctly to the 7 principles, the 7 principles are in fact universal law, my spirit guides were giving me thoughts about the 7 principles, I felt very stongly that the 7 principles should be modernised, as they were communicated to the level of understanding at the time, the 7 principles were communicated to spiritualism through the mediumship of Emma Hardinge Britten in 1871 this is 2014 I thought, understanding of spirit and how the universe interacts with us has changed, they should be reworded so they can be understood by all.

It came time to give the inspired address to the congregation, I stood up and explained that I was very drawn to the 7 principles of spiritualism, but felt they were out of date, and needed to be modernised, not the thing I should be saying in a SNU Church I exclaimed to laughter from the congregation, let us look at the 7 principles of spiritualism from spirits view.

1, The Fatherhood Of God

Today we understand what we call God as a great universal energy and intelligence the creator of all things, yes our father in biblical times but 2000 years later, we should update to oneness or empathy with creation instead of the fatherhood of god.

2, The Brotherhood Of Man

Have women not been created yet (laughter from congregation), when the 7 principles were communicated it was very much a mans world, women did not have the vote and had less rights than a man, now today we live in a age of equality perhaps this principle could be changed, to the unity of the human race, it would be more in keeping with the principle of the brotherhood of man, and would be a modern interpretation of this principle.

3, The Communion Of Spirits And The Ministry Of Angels

As spiritualists this principle is a cornerstone of our knowledge as is eternal life, the word communion by definition, is the sharing of intimate thoughts and feelings on a mental or spiritual level, spirit and angels communicate with us in thoughts and feelings, the universe communicates with us in thoughts feelings and synchronicities, it is not only mediums and healers that have communion with spirits and angels and the universe, everyone can communicate with spirit angels and the universe as we are all interconnected by creation, spirit teach that all things come from one source, and it is this one source that connects us all and everything together, spirit teach that thought is the most powerful thing in our universe, so let us all use our thoughts to communicate with our loved ones spirit guides angels creation and the universe,

Spirit angels creation and the universe will communicate back to us in different ways, but we have to be aware enough to perceive what is coming back to us, this is where spiritual development comes in and teaches us how to communicate on many levels, I feel the third principle could be simplified to universal communication.

4, The Continuous Existence Of The Human Soul

This principle is the spiritualist aim to prove survival the spirit and soul, after physical death and as we all know this truth is on going, but it is not just the human spirit that survives physical death, all that has life has spirit even a rock or a mountain has life and spirit, because everything can be broken down to atoms and atoms have energy, and it is a level of this energy that is spirit, that we have not invented a machine that can measure that energy yet, I feel this principle could be simplified to eternal life.

5, Personal Responsibility

We are all responsible for our thoughts and deeds in life, in this principle it teaches us to take responsibility for our thoughts and actions, how many times have we heard people complain about their lives, when in fact they are the creators of their lives, so they should take responsibility for how their lives turn out, and guide them to change their lives for the better, in universal law we are responsible for our thoughts and deeds as you give so shall you receive, I feel this principle should not be re worded because it is what it is, but I feel should be taught in churches and development circles.

6, Compensation And Retribution Hereafter For All The Good And Evil Deeds Done On Earth

This principle is very much universal karmic law, simply as you give so shall you receive in eternal life, there are many different levels of spirit as above so below, the level we go to in spirit depends on our thoughts and actions here on earth, spirit guides teach that we create heaven or hell in spirit, depending on our thoughts and actions on earth, this teaching should guide us to be loving kind and compassionate in our thoughts and actions here on earth, the truth is we create our own heaven or hell this could be brought up to date to, as you give as you give so shall you receive in eternal life.

7, Eternal Progress Open To Every Human Soul

This principle is very outdated and wrong, all that has life has soul whether human animal plant mineral, animals communicate with us from spirit, we can also communicate with elemental spirits, earth air fire and water all thing, from one source so all things have soul, and it is in this truth we can see the levels of spirit working here on earth, we can progress spiritually here on earth to raise our soul up another level, we can still do so in spirit we can also go backwards, depending on what level we choose to vibrate at through our thoughts and actions, this principle simply needs to be updated to eternal progress open to every soul.

The inspired address appeared to be well received by the congregation, after the next hymn it was time for the demonstration of mediumship, messages from loved ones spirit guides and angels flowed, there were tears and laughter and I was very relieved, as my nervousness told me I would not get anything, after the service three lovely people, Anne Cosh Barbara-Ann Winter and Mark Sloper, told me how much they enjoyed the service as did others, and they recommended me to other churches to serve, the booking secretary was very happy that the service went well as I was unknown to them, but how she got my name and number is still a mystery, but I suspect spirit played a big hand in it, she said she would re book me again but I have heard nothing more from her or the church.

Whatever the reason was for spirit guiding me to Cirencester Spiritualist Church, I do know that I have learned a lot from it, that I am still a medium and spirit wish to communicate through me, a lot of good has come from that service I have made friends and served other churches, and I thank spirit for the blessing of their guidance.

Closer To Spirit

Opening my heart to all that is draws me closer to spirit, I give thanks for the new day, conscious and alive the new day brings blessings in abundance, my mind becomes the open unwritten book, I am the creator within the magical genesis of creation, breeze blowing through the trees connects me to the energy of life, and love and all that is closer to spirit I am aware.

I offer myself in service to all that is, that I may always work towards the greatest and highest good for all, who seek to be closer to spirit, seeking the greatest and highest good from within myself, manifesting unconditional love my heart full to the brim, I walk with spirit a vocation, a calling, my reason for being closer to spirit.

Stephen Rowlands

My Prayer For Protection Answered

I have often spoken about prayer describing prayer as thought, as a lot of people are put off prayer, by the religious connotations of prayer, I find prayer to be a useful tool in my daily life, to help me focus on what I need to do, in a religious sense prayer is our communication with the divine, we pray and a religion created God answers our prayers or not within our own perception, creation in one way or another, interacts with us in lessons to help us achieve what we are praying for, spirit guides have often taught that thought is the most powerful energy in the universe, so thinking about it the energy of our thoughts in prayer, are a real interaction with the life force and energy of creation, that religion calls God.

Our light within communicates and interacts with the source light of creation, through our hearts and minds, how many times have we become at peace after prayer, this is a indication of our light interacting with source light, as we receive thoughts from the source of creation, we can gain guidance from source light, and help us to change our lives for the better, the spiritual journey here on earth, is very much a inner journey to develop light within us, by the lessons we receive from source light, to guide us on our spiritual journey here on earth, I feel inspired to write about my life and prayer at this point in time, to give an example of how our inner light, interacts and communicates with source light and wisdom.

I have been working as a security officer for the past 28 years, in varying roles in that time I have been shot at stabbed with a needle kicked and punched, and suffered various injuries from these assaults, for the past 3 months I have been working as a retail security officer, deterring shoplifters from stealing goods from a well known food retailer, the scene has changed very much from when I was a store detective 12 years ago, it used to be very cat and mouse with shoplifters doing their best to avoid detection, for fear of prosecution, today the police will not respond to shoplifting as it is deemed low level crime, due to government cuts to police and lack of resources, now shoplifters are openly stealing and being violent, if store security or shop staff try to stop or apprehend them, as there is now little or no chance of them being prosecuted and sentenced, my role is becoming more staff protection than being a deterrent to shop thieves.

I must admit at 58 years old this concerns me, as I am not as physically fit, and cannot be as physically aggressive as I used to be, in deterring and arresting shoplifters, for the past couple of weeks I have been working in a store, where assaults on staff are very much on the increase, my role is to visit a different store in that chain every day, but due to assaults at this store on staff by shoplifters, the store has asked for a greater security presence there, on 21/11/18 I arrived at the store and I did not know why, but I felt I should pray and ask for protection for myself and the store that day, at 18.04 hrs a male and female entered the store, who I knew to be shoplifters, he is about 6' 5" tall and powerfully built, and in his mid 20's early thirties, the female is tall and skinny with obvious signs of drug abuse, I walked quickly to the meat section, as I knew they were going to go for the high value steaks, the male walked around to the next section, where the lamb and gammon joints were, the female stood about 5' away from me pretending to browse the ham and burgers, I stood in front of the steak to protect it.

About 20 seconds later the male appeared with his open carrier bag, he said to me "keep out of the way mate this is nothing to do with you" and started to put steaks in his carrier bag, I started to take the steaks from him, telling him they are not his steaks and to leave the store, some pushing and shoving between us ensued, I was pushed back into the chiller but bounced back at him, he kept saying to me "do not touch me" I replied leave the steaks alone, this went on for about 45 – 60 seconds, in the struggle some steaks fell on the floor, and I stood on them to protect them from theft, myself and the male just looked at each other, it was a silent and eerie split second, he could see I was not going to retreat, then he and the female left the store, a manager who had witnessed the incident asked me if I was ok, I dialled 101 and reported the incident to police, also reporting it as a assault on myself as I was pushed into the chiller, knowing the police would give this incident more attention.

23/11/18 a police officer came to the store, to take a statement from me reference the assault on me and the theft of steak from the store, and to seize cctv evidence, the police officer told me that the male I wrestled with, was a nasty piece of work and was involved in a vicious assault on another man, which the man will take several months to recover from, my prayer for protection that day came back into my mind, realising I could have been seriously injured that day or worse, in that eerie split second in the incident, I believe spirit spoke to the male and he made the decision not to harm me and walk away, over giving me a good hiding to allow him to steal the steaks, I am so thankful and grateful to creation angels and spirit guides, for answering my prayer and confirming to me the power of prayer.

My Light

I honour my light my truth and guide

My healer when regret overcomes me

Lessons to learn let me not forget my light

My light protects me against all who persecute me

When all is dark within and around me

Darkness cannot extinguish the light of my being

My light alive and eternal within and without

Created by and born in infinite love

Love is the light the true nature of my existence

I honour spirit thankful for my purpose of service

I honour all who are aware within light

We are one in light and truth

Stephen Rowlands

Ghosts

Inspired to take a walk on this fine sunny autumn day, with all good intentions I walk the canal toe path, to the chrysalis of my beginnings in langley, deeply inhaling the air of life, exhaling the stresses of working life, seeking my better and higher self, I used to walk this path in my youth, to visit friends or to be a marine cadet at T.S. Lion. Revisiting my memories was not my intention, we walk with our memories throughout our lifespan, awaiting in mind to torture or celebrate in heart. Realising it is best to make good memories in the present, so my memories of now, will not become a heavy burden in the future. The autumn sun shines brightly magnifying the colours of autumn leaves, the landscape has changed around here, there are now businesses and homes along the canal, where once were fields

The peace and beautiful serenity of nature brings vibrant energy to my soul, in stark contrast to the industrial town that surrounds it, man and mother nature reside together happily in this place, we the human race are mother nature's children, she gave birth to us all, we are her spoiled children as we take from her, and pollute our mothers love. Walking up the path to the bridge the Deseronto Wharf, where I once worked at Bryce Whites Timber Yard, has now gone but the office building has survived time, Lindley Thompsons is now a business park, walking over the railway bridge, I stand with my memories, back in time looking at the place I once called home.

Perhaps this is the purpose of my journey today, to revisit my past and make peace with my memories, I see my nan looking out of the window, waiting for me to come home for lunch, The Gulley where we once played now flattened, swings and roundabouts now replace rusty old cars, the giants hill, the three wise old apple trees. Old Hobi the tramp who slept in Grandads pigsty, old nelson the chicken who we loved and ate one Sunday, my Grandad owned the gulley my Dad, family, and friends, built our bungalow, a great place to grow up and I feel blessed to have grown here. The Chesntuts pub across the road the social hub of our community, where we drank to celebrate our success or maudlin in our sorrows, my classroom from boy to man, as I walk down St Marys Road, I see myself as a schoolboy walking with mum for my first day at Langley Marish School. The Almshouses built in 1649 where my dad did maintenance, a ceiling collapsed revealing the original mud and horse hair ceiling, and a rusty 17th century 9 inch nail, St Marys Church so many memories of family and friends weddings, christenings, and funerals.

I visit my nan and grandads grave, telling them of my life and wishing they were still with us, I would love to know what they think of me now, so many emotions and memories swirling within me, that I did not realise I could feel and see all this at once, I stop by The Chestnuts for a drink, no one did I know or recognise for we are all old now, realising now that time has passed and I am now a stranger, in the place I once called home. Night has nearly fallen as I walk the canal toe path, to the place I now call home, the love of spirit embraces me reminding me, that ghosts are memories, spirit is eternal, our home is with God, and in time all things change in our world.

YesterYear

To dwell within the moment is fine living, within the moment my mind awakens alive in yesteryear, to the people who I love and have passed away in time, sunshine on leafy trees with gentle breeze, aware my heart with all its love, to know that I was loved, but knowing in the now yesteryear has passed, but the love still remains, of all the people I love who have passed away in time.

Jesus: The Man Saving Us From Ourselves By Teaching Universal life and Love

God within me God without, how shall I ever be in doubt,
I am the sower and the sown, God's self unfolding own.

Meister Eckhart

As a Christian Spiritualist, Jesus is the one true example of all I know to be the truth. He was a soul living an earthly life through a physical body, and a material world. He was fully aware of his soul connection to the source, that we have named God. He was also a medium and healer, and when he died his spirit left his body and went into spirit, so what makes Jesus so different to me, or any of us, I believe it is now the time to really change our perception of ourselves. As I have long realised he was the personification of us all, his message was very simple I am you. And we can all develop the same love, compassion, kindness, as Jesus by knowing he came to show the human race who we truly are.

We are souls living and learning through a human experience, this is what I believe he was teaching us, when he said, "I am the way the truth and the life. No one comes to the father except through me" Jesus is an ascended master do we really think that he wanted to be worshipped, with worship it focusses all the goodness and divinity onto him, and makes us blind to our own goodness and divinity, and to his teachings, distracting us from developing his teachings from within, making us the hopeless sinners we are led to believe we are by organised religion.   I feel strongly to say he wanted us to listen to him, and learn from him, about the truth of our existence here on mother earth, and to our soul connection to what we have named God, and for his teachings to be passed down through the ages. By doing this the consciousness and vibration of the human race, would have been raised to a much higher level, collectively and individually, this I believe was the purpose of Jesus being here on earth, he was actually trying to save us from ourselves, but through religion we have totally missed the point of the teaching and lessons. Religion is great for souls to come together, to share support and grow together, but sadly it has been corrupted by mans need for power and control.

Jesus had his troubles and temptations here in his short earthy life as we do, yet throughout his life he taught and guided us, how to deal with our problems, this is Jesus man and teacher, he dealt with his problems with love and intuition, at times he did not have the answers so he prayed, he asked for guidance and direction, as we do when we are lost, he was tempted by the devil out in the desert, for strength to resist temptation he prayed, and in doing so he was attuning himself, to the source of his being that we have named God, and in doing so attuning himself to his higher self, in his life story the source was identified as his father, I know the source to be the father and mother of us all depending on your perspective of the source. I really feel strongly to say it is wrong to believe, that Jesus was the son of God, in fact he was our brother, teaching us of our connection to the source throughout his life, to believe Jesus was the son of God, makes him some kind of supernatural being, within our human biological mind set.

When in truth Jesus was exactly the same as us, mind, body, spirit, soul, living an earthly existence to experience, learn, give, and grow. To look on Jesus as a supernatural being, is now very old hat and wrong we have to remember that Jesus, was communicating to people 2000 years ago , so the source through him was communicating to the level of understanding at the time, we now live in a time of science and technology, it's about time our understanding of life and spirituality, moved along with the times, but man made religion likes to keep us in our place, so we remain its servants via a man made supernatural being, and making us feel incapable of attaining, what Jesus taught us what is naturally within us. When Jesus spoke of his fathers house I strongly believe, he was talking of what we believe is heaven, or as I believe the spirit world, the many mansions he spoke of, to me are the many many levels of spirit within the spirit world, nobody knows how many levels there are, as there are many lives and existences we know nothing about, it is a massive universe we live in.   Jesus said he would prepare a place for us, I really do not believe Jesus meant as religion tells us, that we have to believe in him or the man made religion that adopted him, to gain a place with him in heaven or the spirit world, the place he would be preparing for us would be defined by, the life we led here on earth by our thoughts and actions, as to the kind of room that would be prepared for us. My house has many mansions means to me, that there is room for all, our thoughts and actions here on earth dictate, whether we land up living eternally in a palace, or a slum, a nice maisonette, a council estate, or suburbia. Our level of spirit is dictated by our soul progression, again by our thoughts and actions here on earth, we can as souls go up and down the levels of spirit, depending on our thoughts and actions, the choice is ours Jesus was guiding us to choose love, kindness, and compassion, over hatred, anger, selfishness , ignorance. We all have the universal gift of freewill, so we should make our choices wisely, freewill is the engine of spirit and soul development, let us make the template for our lives the teachings of Jesus, and all the other ascended masters, because they all brought the same message to us, the truth has one source but many different teachers, depending on our level of understanding.

Jesus life was teaching us the universal way of life, but in doing so he upset the religion of the time, because he was teaching us that we are responsible for our lives, and how we live it and not as a servant to man made religion, and in doing so taking away the power that religion had over the people. He upset the local government which were the romans at that time, by the amount of people that were following Jesus teachings, they feared civil unrest with the possibility of being overthrown. At this time we see Jesus the man, living life by his freewill and choices, because his teachings were love, I honestly do not believe he realised how much upset, he was causing, he was upsetting religion and government, the two most powerful factions of the time and still are to this day. On his crucifixion Jesus said "father forgive them for they know not what they do" but they knew exactly what they were doing, they were getting rid of a trouble maker, because of the collective ego, they did not want to lose their power, they chose that over change and progression, to a better way of life, yes they were driven by greed. I do not believe Jesus wanted to die that day, as he prayed and asked his father for help to live, religion tells us that Jesus died to save us from sin, again making him supernatural but it was the sin of greed that killed him. We have to take the teachings of universal and unconditional love within, make them our living and speaking truth through heart, then Jesus death would not have been in vain, whether you believe Jesus existed or not, it's a great story that can heal guide and uplift us.

Conscious Within Christ light

I sit down to pray in my dark room, visualising a white cross, to focus my love for healing, I find myself floating in the stars, looking down on mother earth, a jewel in the crown of creation, in awe of the starlight the realisation comes, I am floating in Christ light, it is still and silent the permanance of eternity, nothing can shatter this connection to all things, no ripples can disturb this divine space.

At one and conscious within Christ light, I must still my mind for the message to be heard, and understood in heart, he never came to free us from sin, he came to show us we are eternal, to look beyond ourselves to see our need for wealth status and power, are of little relevance in eternal life, he was not a saviour he came to guide us, to know the starlight Christ light is within us all, my heart now illumined in star Christ light, is the gift and knowledge he came to share.

Stephen Rowlands

Meditation

Over the years I have asked many people if they meditate, because I feel it could help them, or spirit feels it would help them to meditate, mostly I get the same answer. It's too difficult, my mind wanders , I have too much on my mind to meditate, I have not got the time to meditate. So I have decided to write this blog, to outline a simple way to meditate. Meditation is a great way to relax and focus our minds, to find answers to questions, or to calm turbulent thoughts and emotions. The first thing I was taught about meditation, is you cannot have imagination without an image, so meditation is simply day dreaming. And that is something we all do, but unlike day dreaming where our minds create the mental images we would like, such as winning the lottery, or getting a date with a film or pop star, being with someone we miss, or our penchant for looking back into the past, and the many what ifs that arise from mentally living in the past, our minds create the mental images of the most satisfying possibilities. Meditation is in fact focussed day dreaming, whereby we mentally get the image we want, within our minds eye and allow everything else to take place without our input. A good starting meditation is to imagine yourself sitting alone on a beach, on a warm sunny day mentally put yourself on the beach, focus on smelling the sea air, hearing the waves lapping on the shore, watching seagulls flying above the waves, what other sights, sounds, and senses are you aware of. We only need to meditate for a few minutes to get the benefit of it. Being perfect at meditation is not the point of meditation, levitating our minds to a more peaceful, higher level of awareness is the aim of meditation. We are exercising mental muscles we don't often use. But like any exercise, the more we do it the better we get at it, if we are distracted by other thoughts. Like work, or what to have for dinner, financial and emotional worries, discard those thoughts let them pass and get back to your beach the more frequently you meditate, I suggest 2 or 3 times a week, distractions will become less and less. A simple exercise I use to prepare for meditation, to help focus my thoughts, is what is known as stepping into the moment, this is what I find best do, and works for me.

1, Find a comfy chair make yourself comfortable

2, Shut your eyes and inhale through your nose, and gently exhale from your mouth, this helps relax our muscles and stimulates our minds, to a slightly higher state of awareness, to prepare for meditation.

3, Realise it is only us that makes the noise with our thoughts and feelings, sit quietly and realise that you have peace and tranquillity all around you. It is only us that makes the noise so put your thoughts and feelings to one side, it does not matter if a bomb is falling on your house, step into the peace and tranquillity of the moment. This can also be difficult to achieve, but the more we practice meditation we will find it easier to be in the moment.

4, Once in the moment or your feeling more relaxed, remember to discard any day to day thoughts, worries. anxieties, aches and pains. Not easy to do but practice makes perfect, I have been meditating for years, and still get distracted but don't be disheartened, just get back to the image you started with.

Now you're ready to visualise where you want to be, it can be anywhere but make sure it is a positive image, like sitting on a beach, or walking down a path in the forest, focus on what you can see. hear, sense, smell, within your image dont tamper with it let it play like a movie. Meditation teaches us and helps us to discover our trueselves, other than what we have conditioned ourselves to become. Helping us to become a better version of ourselves so honesty with ourselves is a priceless tool in meditation.

Journey

The journey of my life is my lesson

I have never failed in my life

I am learning the truth of my soul

Failure teaches us what we are not

Gently guiding us to our innermost truth

Stephen Rowlands

Humility

In my weakness I embraced humility and it became my greatest strength, and in my strength I found my truth, a child of creation born from the stars, as all are creation, no greater than the sky no lower than the dirt, gifted and flawed acceptance of myself and others is my virtue, and by the grace of creation go I, on mother earth I stand reaching out to the sky and stars above, balance in heart and mind, with humility as my guide.

Fill Your Hearts With Love

I went along one evening to a spiritual development circle, run by my friend Kevin Trefry, he said to me you're not going to sit there and do nothing, I want you to give the meditation. I was a bit put out by this as I was very tired, and in need of recharging, I just wanted to just sit and enjoy the closeness of spirit. And do some of the mediumship exercises with the students, as I feel it is important to keep developing, and to maintain and strengthen our links with spirit, so I asked my spirit guides, what would be the best meditation to give to the circle. My spirit guide Jerome a Franciscan Monk came forward, and said ask them, to draw unconditional love from God into their hearts, to fill their hearts with unconditional love.

After the opening prayer I asked the students, to visualise the love of God, coming from above in white light, filling their hearts with divine unconditional love. The meditation began, myself and Kevin watched over the students, after 10 minutes or so I called the students back from their meditation, and I asked them each in turn, what they experienced during the meditation, and they all felt very empowered, and a great connection to all things, The lesson in the meditation is that love is the power of all things and is our connection to all things, the next day Jerome came to me, and inspired me with a poem, from the previous night's meditation.

Fill Your Hearts With Love

Eternally flowing in abundance from our soul source.

Gentle as a friendly smile, powerful as the sun.

Divine in thought, sacred in action.

Creedless colourless, love connects all.

Love is freedom, from fear and doubt.

Egoless non physical, unconditional love is.

Communicated to Stephen Rowlands by Spirit Guide Jerome 30th May 2016

Fast forward to 22/10/17, I was inspired to give Jerome's poem as a reading at the divine service Jennings Street Christian Spiritualist Church Swindon. The poem was well received by those in attendance, Jerome then went on to inspire me with the address from the poem, he inspired me to say that love is a choice, as everything in life is a choice, out of the vast range of emotions that we can feel, love is the emotion that we rarely choose, when we are faced with some form of adversity or negativity in life. We tend to rely on our base instincts such as anger, confusion, jealousy, a loss of self worth. When people are horrible to us, or we make a mistake in life through our choices in life, all this comes from our ego our pride kicks in, and we react seeking to hurt those who have hurt us, or anger when our plans go wrong, making the situation worst for ourselves and those around us.

Let us step onto the back foot rather than reacting with hurt, let us seek the solution to our problems with love, and ask ourselves what is the best solution to this problem with love, rather than always choosing our base instinct ego, to solve our problems, causing greater disharmony to the spirit of ourselves and others, when we think feel and act with love, we are connecting to our higher selves, our soul the true part of us, that lives within what we call God, whilst our spirit lives and learns through our minds and bodies, in this material world of the earth plane. Love is a great spectrum of all emotion, at its lowest level we have hatred, anger, greed, jealousy, avarice, sloth. at its highest level there is divine unconditional love.

We spirits who live and learn in this physical and material world, find ourselves going up and down the sliding scale, of the emotional spectrum of love, let love be our choice in all things, to heal our hurt feelings and calm negative situations, let love be our guide, not only with family and friends, but in all things and with all peoples, and in doing so we are putting ego in its place, and making life better for ourselves and all around us, helping us to find the inner peace we so often crave, when I first got into spiritualism, I was taught it is a big part of our spiritual development, to turn negative into positive that is why we are faced with negativity and adverse conditions at times, I truly believe we are here to learn how to love, that is our spiritual purpose for being here, the ascended masters who teach through the religions who adopted them, they all teach love its about time we all pricked up our ears, listened to the teachings of love from the masters, take those teachings within ourselves and live them, because surely we are all fed up with the terrible things that are going on around us and in the world, it needs us to make love, kindness, compassion, tolerance, Our way of life and truth.

Whilst writing this fill your hearts with love, I was taken back to the time when I used to sit on the back doorstep, at home in Langley my nan would be cooking Sunday dinner. I would be writing inspired notes for the address for the service that night, I have walked through 2 dark nights of the soul in life, and in the dark night I missed those times, but feel very blessed right now those times are now back. With me so I say to all who feel they are walking in darkness, be true to yourself, love yourself, love life no matter how dark it gets, and the sun will rise again.

NAMASTE

LOVE IS THE ENERGY OF
THE UNIVERSE
AND IS THE CREATOR OF
ALL THINGS

Love Is My Teacher

When darkness befalls me
Love teaches me to be light
When I feel unloved
Love teaches me to love
When I feel persecuted
Love teaches me to live my truth
When I am hurt
Love teaches me to speak my truth
When I feel all is gone
Love teaches me to open my heart
Love is my guide in this mortal life
Love teaches me
The truth of my eternal soul

Inspired by Spirit

Stephen Rowlands 26/11/19

Healer Heal Thyself Diabetes 2

The Kick Up The Ass I Needed

Where do I begin this part of my biography, from the beginning I suppose, but hard to remember where it all began, but thinking about it was a long downward slope of around 18 years, in that time I had 3 long-term girlfriends, one who I adored cheated on me, the pain of her infidelity took me from 16 stone 10 pounds to 12 stone, the next girlfriend thought I was the Royal Bank of Mug but laced it up as love, by that time I was drinking heavily and smoking around 40-60 cigarettes a day.

And to be honest my life was at rock bottom at that point, although I was working full-time and had a flat, I was scratching around spiritually and no social life, and I was skint so on boxing day 2010, I decided I needed to turn my life around, and make 2011 a year of change, and started getting myself out there as once upon a time in the mid 80's to early 90's, I was a spiritualist medium demonstrating mediumship at spiritualist churches, on what we call the circuit I missed those times, I had spoken to my spirit guides saying to them I was fed up, with getting into relationships and landing up with nothing, they advised me to do what I was good at to work with them and be a medium and healer once again.

I became friends with a lovely lady and fellow medium Jane Lorraine Goodman, who helped me to see the errors of my ways with drinking and smoking, and holding onto anger due to past hurts, drinking smoking and being a temperamental sod, that had a very real detrimental effect on me as a channel for spirit. so I weaned myself off the booze from drinking daily to drinking occasionally, as I enjoy a glass of wine or beer when out for dinner or a few drinks when at parties, so I decided not to drink in the week or 24 hours before serving spirit, much better for me to drink socially, than to be in a pissed or hung over state by drinking daily.

I smoked for 40 years so giving up was not going to be easy, so I got the patches and nicotine lozenges, and kicked the habit but I must admit to my shame, today I am still addicted to the nicotine lozengers, and do enjoy the occasional fag but when I do I think why am I doing this, it stinks and its horrible but hey ho it's all part of the psyche of being a bad non smoker, my mediumship is much improved by getting drinking and smoking under control, and my general well-being is much improved to as getting my drinking under control has really helped me deal with my anger issues, and booze really changes you into a not nice person, and with meditation and practising what I preach, I am much more at peace with myself others and the world. So in 2011 I found myself single I had not been single for 14 years, I began getting used to my own company, and getting to know and love myself, new year 2011 was an incredibly positive time for me, thinking back being single was the best thing that had happened to me for years, I realised I had got my life back to rebuild and customise my life for me, you may find that a very selfish statement, but I very much-needed my life, back to develop into all I could and can become.

This development will continue until the day I physically die, For the first time in 14 years I did not have a girlfriend to cook for me, you may not believe this but at nearly 51 years old I did not know how to cook, except like basic things like a boiled egg a fry up a cup of tea sandwiches etc etc etc, you get my drift with working 12 hour rotating day and night shifts, I was too lazy and had no inclination to learn how to cook for myself, so for my main meal I would eat a Tescos finest ready meal with 4 slices of white bread and Bertolli spread, breakfast would be porridge Weetabix or corn flakes with semi skimmed milk or a fry up, lunch would be 2 rounds of mature cheddar sandwiches with crisps or chocolate, and 2 rounds of sandwiches crisps and chocolate for nightshift.

The weight began to pile on I thought it did not matter, as I was in my mid 50's my handsome hunk days were over, I became impotent which hurt as in my mind I still considered myself as a red-blooded male, but I thought hey ho the ladies are not interested in me anymore, I had lost teeth on my upper and lower sets and had become obese, this now seems a funny way of thinking to me, now as I love female company, most of my friends are ladies I just thought of it all as an age thing, but with what I know now I realise I had let myself go big time, and was not caring for myself as I should, I have spent a lot of time over the years talking to people about the importance of loving oneself, I have now realised I need to practice what I have been preaching with self love, over the past few years I have been working to let go of all past hurts, and my anger re past hurts again, as I thought practising what I preach, but throughout all that I had omitted to care for my physical wellbeing.

The symptoms of Diabetes 2 came on slowly between 2011 - March 2016, constantly feeling tired and lethargic wanting to sleep all the time, an itchy red rash on my ankles and shins taking ages to pee, which I thought at the time maybe a prostrate problem, feeling like I had a bag of sugar in my mouth, and impotence my mum would also tell me I smelt funny, but since my diet she says the smell has gone, I can only put this down to all the crap I was eating, I have realised it is very true we are what we eat, I decided to finally address my health issues in March 2016, and got a doctor's appointment, I told the doctor my health problems did a blood and urine test I was called back into see the doctor 07/04/16 she told me my testosterone was fine, but I was full of sugar with a sugar score of 63 (7.9) I was in fact suffering from Diabetes 2, and all my health problems were related to Diabetes 2 and my weight, the 5ft nothing doctor then proceeded to give me the mother of all telling offs, of the state I had got myself into, and at my age and weight I was at very high risk of a heart attack or stroke, and I needed to do something about it pronto. By losing weight eating diabetic friendly foods and a lot more exercise the doctor prescribed metformin to treat the diabetes 2 and statins for my borderline cholesterol score the doctor advised I may get a upset stomach with the metformin but I actually found the metformin to be a help to my diet because it helped me to lose weight quickly as the metformin took all the crap out of my body pardon the pun :-) I was then dispatched to see the diabetic nurse another 5ft nothing terror who then proceeded to give me another telling off about my state and gave me a check up my stats didn't look to good that day weight 17 stone 7 pounds waist 49 inches Qrisk (lifescore) 20.92% the lower that score is the better Diabetes 63 (7.9) my blood pressure was also very high which was a shock to me as I have always had good blood pressure I could only put this down to the Tesco finest meals I had been shoving in my face since 2011 as they are full of salt and sugar I threw my ready meals out as soon as I got home.

I promised the diabetic nurse I would lose weight, she told me she didn't think I would be able to do it, I thought lock and load bitch you watch, thinking about it that was a great thing to say to me, and it really helped motivate me, so I went home and called my closest friend Marina, I told her what had happened at the doctors and in true Marina form she said I need to diet I will diet with you, I admitted to her I didn't know how to cook she said she will teach me the basics, and she would visit Sunday 10/04/16 we would go shopping and go for a walk, show me how to cook mince and veg, I went back to the nurse 14/04/16, and my blood pressure had returned to normal, and that was just in a week of not eating ready meals, just goes to show how unhealthy they are On the 10/04/16 my diet began, but this diet needed to be different as I had spent most of my adult life dieting, then putting the weight back on over the past couple of years, I had started dieting but lacked the motivation or willpower to continue dieting, so I needed to lose the weight and maintain it, being told by the doctor and nurse, that my life expectancy was not that good if I didn't change my ways, lose weight and control my diabetes was a real motivation to lose weight, after reading the diabetes literature basically I had to eat meat or fish with veg for main meals, cut way down on my carbs I love bread and potatoes, but surprisingly it was easy to do and cut down on dairy foods, I absolutely love eggs and cheese so this was hard, and I very much missed cheese throughout my diet, and the fact that I have a very low metabolism, which means when I diet I have to eat very little to lose weight.

On the 22/08/16 I went for a blood test, I was really hoping my blood sugar score would be 48 or below, that would mean I become be a diet controlled diabetic, on the 23/08/16 I received a phone call from the diabetic nurse, my blood sugar score was now 31 I could either come off the metformin, or take just one a day so I opted to come off metformin, as I was concerned about the long term effect it would have on my body, I kicked the statins into touch as well, she said she wanted to see me urgently so I made an appointment with her for that afternoon, I entered her office and she said to me I can see you have been wasting away, I said told you I could do it she looked at me blankly, but I had a great feeling of satisfaction growing within me, she gave me a check up my stats looked much better that day, weight 14 stone 1 pound waist 36 inches Diabetes 31 Qrisk (lifescore) 18.51%.

FOCUS AND INTENTION

I realised I needed to be totally focussed on my goal of losing 4 stone in weight, so I made a promise to myself that I would lose 4 stone in weight, as I knew this would help to keep me focussed on my goal, as I did not want the feeling of letting myself down if I failed to lose weight, I also started a Facebook page titled Stevieboys Diet and Positive Way of Life page, to chart my progress on my diet and share positive quotes, but mainly I didn't want to make myself look stupid in front of my facebook friends, and that to would help me to stay focussed I achieved my 4 stone weight loss 23/10/16, 13 stone 7 pounds I feel so much fitter and happier and have alot more energy, to I am currently working down to 12 stone 7 pounds as the doctor tells me that is the right weight for my height and build. Dieting should not be seen as a chore or as self torture when in actual fact it is self care, the whole mind set about dieting really needs to change, from being torture to self care and it is all part of loving yourself, taking care of your body is all about self love and care, we buy a warm coat to keep out the cold in winter time, the same could be said about dieting, we care for ourselves to stay healthy and to keep out illness.

Wishing For My Willpower

During the course of my diet, people would say to me I wish I had your willpower to stick to a diet, I found this a very weak and defeatist statement to make, and why were these people belittling themselves, when in fact willpower lives and breathes within in us all, a state of consciousness when properly utilised can help us to, become the best version of ourselves in any area of our life, or all of it our willpower is usually hidden under many things positive and negative in nature, usually our needs the things that make this life more bearable such as food alcohol cigarettes drugs, relationships a job that drains us a toxic relationship, how we see ourselves in our world, and how we fit into our world our fears and anxieties, and what we use to salve our emotions to deal with life, whilst thinking about writing this piece I realised that willpower is in all things that we do, from our waking moment until we sleep, we just cover it with lots of other things, which really impedes or stops dead our freewill, to use our natural God given willpower, We just really need to reprogram ourselves to look at what we really truly need, and let go of the things that impede or stop us reaching inner peace or desired goals, no matter what they maybe people places thoughts and emotions, if they no longer serve us for our greater good and life they must go, I have realised I have hit on a massive subject, of which scientists and philosophers have researched over centuries.

I can only speak from my own experience along my pathway of life, and the teachings of spirit, so please you the reader do not look at this piece as a piece of academic work, this piece is purely from my own experience and discoveries of self, that I will be sharing with you I will endeavour to make this piece, as helpful as possible and hope you the reader will gain something from it, to utilise and reboot you're in built willpower, and use it towards your inner peace and desired goals. On reflection I realise it was not only the threat of more serious illness, and worsening diabetes that motivated me and helped me to find my willpower, from 2011 - 2016 I had been dieting on and off without any success, but my way of thinking at the time was really suppressing my willpower, the guilt that I had failed another diet the thoughts that it did not really matter, as I was in my mid 50's my pulling the ladies days were over, my absence of teeth and my impotence made me feel useless, my aches and pains and tiredness were just ageing, but putting all these things together they were suppressing my willpower, You may find this hard to believe but when diagnosed with Diabetes 2, I was in the best place mentally and emotionally than I had been for years, after my ex girlfriend ended our relationship in 2010, I was a mess mentally and emotionally and drinking heavily, but realised soon after that I had got my life back, which is a great gift and it was up to me to create the best life I could for myself, and started the long process of letting go of my anger learning to love myself, and opening my heart and living and speaking my truth through an open heart, I was to wrapped up in what I used to be a serving medium, doing around 100 services a year plus teaching and touring Spiritualist Churches in South Wales, a lot of people back in the day used to call me the peoples medium, because of my down to earth approach whilst demonstrating on platform, a fact I am very proud of to this day, and it made me very angry that I couldn't go back to how it was, and just pick up where I left off, it's a very true saying amongst platform mediums, that you're as good as your last service.

Only as high as I reach, can I grow
Only as far as I seek, can I go
Only as deep as I look, can I see
Only as much as I dream, can I be.

Slowly but surely the realisation came that it does not really matter, what I used to do in the past, all that matters is what I'm doing now, and what I'm doing to create a better tomorrow, so I focussed on my mental and emotional state, forgiving myself and others for bad deeds done, my good friend Jane Goodman kept telling me I have a beautiful heart, so I put my best foot forward and decided to truly love myself, anyone who knows me knows that I'm truly a big softy, and that I am giving and helpful, I as I had cut way back on my drinking it made my thinking that much clearer, and was much easier to be truly who I am without, my mind being shrouded by the thick fog of alcohol, I and gradually my mediumship started to improve. meditation helped me to become more at peace with myself.

And gave me the drive to become a better mental and emotional version of myself, I was making friends I had also started teaching mediumship, in a general development circle at Woking Spiritualist Church, as I told the students in that circle I have made all the mistakes, I am just helping you not to make them, I had created a website for my mediumship, and was doing a few more platform demonstrations of mediumship, that is enough about my mediumship for now, although it did inspire me to write this book about my spiritual journey, I was diagnosed with Diabetes 2 on 07/04/16, although this was a shock my Spirit Guides were telling me I had Diabetes, I kept an open mind on it but hoping I didn't have diabetes, the doctor and nurse told me in no uncertain terms if I did not do the work necessary, to improve my health and wellbeing, my health would deteriorate greatly and possibly an early death, me and my closest friend Marina had been talking and making plans, about travelling together seeing historical sites, and seeing the world the thought of being too ill to travel was totally unacceptable, or to die before my spiritual service on this earth was fulfilled, was totally unacceptable to me, I decided it was a straight fight between me and Diabetes 2, and thus my willpower was reignited and had come alive again, I am so glad that my mental and emotional state had improved as I am sure, if I had not took the steps to improve my mental and emotional state, the state of inertia that I was in coupled with diabetes 2, my health would have deteriorated greatly, but now I had reasons to live and sure as hell Diabetes 2, was not going to stand in my way, I now realise I had got rid of all the rubbish that covered my willpower and held me back to life.

Your Mind Is Your Instrument Learn To Be Its Master And Not Its Slave

Apart from losing weight my diet gave me some realisations, the biggest one being dieting is about self care not self denial or battling hunger until your next meal, when you truly realise you are actually caring for yourself through diet, dieting becomes that much easier, and believe it or not I gradually found dieting to be a pleasure rather than a chore, as I was improving my health and wellbeing I will share my realisations with you, as they all promote strong and powerful willpower.

1, Positive balances Negative in our universe, we are greatly affected by our environment as to how we feel inside, and what decisions that we make by our work and relationships, and so on if we feel low we are more likely to eat unhealthy food, because for a time it makes us feel better for a short time, but in reality we are piling on the pounds and polluting our bodies, so we must balance negative thoughts and emotions with positive thoughts and emotions, for example you hate your job, instead of hating your job look at it as a means of paying your bills, so you can live in a material world, count your blessings as there are many that are far worse off than us, I know thinking like this certainly cheers me up, if you have had a bad day don't moan and gripe about it, and reach for the dairy milk chocolate or wine, think how you could have improved your day, think that tomorrow is a blank page, I have the opportunity and the power of creation to make it a good day, meditate step into the moment because there is truly peace all around us, take a hot shower and visualise washing all that negativity down the plug hole.

2, Craving food I know from past experience cravings for our favourite food, can be intense there is something that is known as state dependant learning, I picked this little gem up from my behavioural neuro pharmacologist ex wife, it is quite simply our brain and body has got used to what we put into it, and the amounts we put into it, and when we lessen the amount, our brain and body starts to crave that amount of food alcohol cigarettes or drugs, we put into it know when you start to diet, the cravings will be fierce but as time goes by they will become less and less, know that and your willpower will be strong, do not fear or succumb to your cravings they will become less, just be determined enough to see it through.

3, A little mental trick I used to use and still do at times, whilst shopping I would see the foods I loved, such as cheese white bread sausages chocolate and pies, and knew they were harmful to my diet and harmful to me, with my diabetes so I would just imagine a skull and crossbones on them, and walk by this helped me stay on the straight and narrow, and realising it was a mental tool for turning a negative into a positive, and helped me beat my cravings thus promoting my willpower.

4, Set yourself goals, thinking about all the weight you need to lose can seem an insurmountable task, I set myself half stone targets which were far easier to reach, than thinking of the whole 4 stone target I originally set for myself, be determined be stubborn with yourself if necessary, as there is always someone who will want you to have dessert or a chip sandwich, saying this once won't hurt, I let nothing detract me from my next half stone target, as it would slow my progress and this will help to exercise, your mental and emotional muscles and strengthen your willpower, when I reached my half stone target, I gave myself a little treat such as a sausage sandwich, it gives us something to aim for and promotes a sense of achievement.

As your clothes start to feel loose try on the clothes that don't fit anymore, then you have a good guide on how much more you need to lose to fit into them clothes, make it a goal to be able to wear them clothes comfortably, I cannot tell you the sense of achievement I had, when I could finally wear my grey suit comfortably, 36" waist small trousers 46" chest.

5. Focus on your goals let nothing detract you from your goals, remember your reprogramming yourself so focus is very important, it will boost your willpower to help you achieve your goals.

6, Intention set your intention to lose your weight, and reach your desired weight, I made myself a promise that I would lose 4 stone in weight, I did not want the guilt of failing to lose 4 stone this set my intention.

I hope you the reader has enjoyed reading this, and have gained some helpful advice from it, I am now the healthiest I have been in years, simply by changing the way I think with focus and intention, and this awoke my willpower.

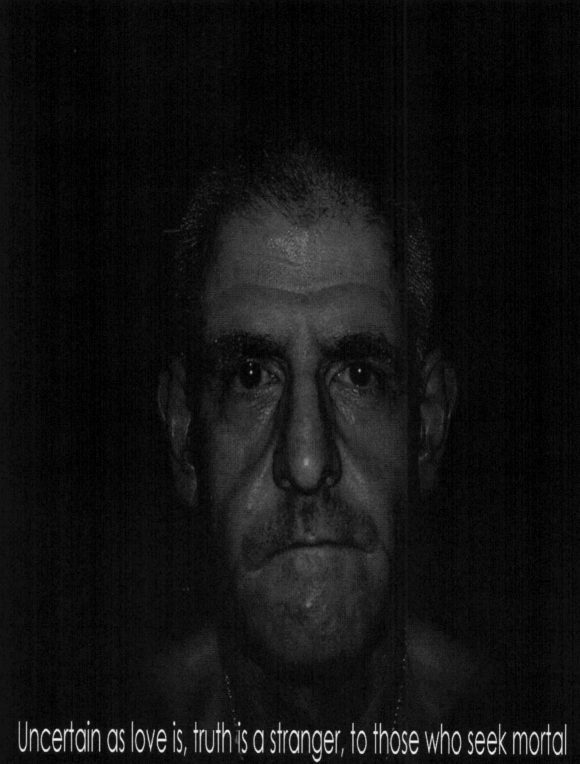

Uncertain as love is, truth is a stranger, to those who seek mortal flesh, but chide union and companionship of mind, The truth I seek in the darkness alone.

Sleep the sleep of angels my love

The beast of the night is now slain

And you banished me to search again

So sleep the sleep of angels my love

Saviour or sinner I loved you

Stephen Rowlands

Shine My Light

My spirit born into this physical life, to experience all emotions to live and learn how to love. It has not been easy for this fish out of water, to live this physical earthly life, programmed from birth to be like everyone else, blessed and burdened with the gifts of spirit, I was the round hole trying to fit the square peg, now I see it was all a waste of time, the peg would never fit   I would have fared much better, if I had just been me focussing on my truth and not lived the lie, I was not meant to be like everyone else.

No longer will I hide my darkness behind my light, I will live in my truth and power and accept all that is within me. I am an Angel and a Demon my legacy in this life has been insight, healing, kindness, compassion, hurt, and pain, for the hurt and pain I have caused please forgive me, to those who have caused me hurt and pain, I forgive you all that matters is here within the now. I was sent to this earth to be a blessing to many, through my foolishness I wasted many a year, searching for what I am not, to you Great Spirit I apologise, to the mothers of my children I apologise, to my two sons who I left behind, I never ever stopped loving you and never will, I fought my battles loved and lost.

Realising to seek acceptance from family and peers is the journey of the fool, when acceptance of the gifted self, is the wisdom of the seeking heart and mind, many regrets have chained me down from the past, the deceivers lies slashing at my heart, finding solace in booze and speed did not comfort my heart only to amplify my bitter rage, as the hungry maggot gnawed at my guts. Living life at each end of the spectrum,, giving messages from spirit teaching mediumship, working the door drinking fighting, No longer will I listen to my demons lies, freeing me of the chains of regret, I hear the gentle loving whisper of my angel within, telling me to shine my light for all to see.

Stephen Rowlands

Dark Night Of My Soul

My soul condemned to this dark night
I shiver with the cold of exile
No one knows of my pain and hurt
Words cannot my mouth make
I walk alone through my dark night of the soul
Torment anger bitterness is the storm
Poisoning my being stifling my peaceful will
And now alone I must suffer for my anger
In heart and mind my soul seeks solace
From your treacherous sarcasm
Seeking freedom from your spiteful possession
You took your wicked cold hearted revenge
I will walk this dark night of my soul
Healing heart and mind to live again
I can no longer wait for the sun to rise
As reason tells me I am a fool to fight your darkness
My salvation from this dark night will be
When my anger no longer gives you power over me
I must journey through this dark night of my soul
Guided by the truth and light of my soul

Stephen Rowlands

When All You Can See Is Darkness

Allow The Radiant Light

Of Your Love

To Shine From Within

Stephen Rowlands

Prayer Lights The Way
Within The Darkest Mind

Stephen Rowlands

My Prayer

Spirit of light and all creation I am your servant

You have taught me to be selfless in your service

Guide me in your truth help me to focus on my path

Grant me strength when I am weary in your service

Guide me to live and speak my truth with love

May I treat all souls with love and compassion

May I be a healer for the sick

May I be a light for people in darkness

May I be love when there is hate

May I be peace when there is anger

May I be a comfort to people who are sad

May I be a friend to the lonely

May I bring calm to the confused

May I speak the wisdom of spirit

Spirit of light and all creation

May my actions express your will through service

For all my days on earth Amen

Stephen Rowlands

I Am Me

Some people say I am lazy
Some people call me crazy
Some fear some hold me dear
After All I Am Me
He has cut his hair
He does not care
He would not dare
After All I Am Me
He has put on weight
He is always late
He has lost weight
After All I Am Me
He thinks to much
He drinks to much
After All I Am Me
I know who I am now
It is all in the past
Today you still cannot grasp
That I am becoming Me
Look at yourselves
And as you delve
You will find the God
Who knows Me
Who are you.

Blessing

Gazing through my window clouds journey silently by, I lie here in awe of the magical consciousness of love and life, freewill in heart and mind is my journey of experience, a blessing to love live and evolve, a beautiful teaching the human race has yet to embrace.

All consciousness is born of love within this universal creation, our consciousness is a gift of love to life, we are the consciousness of love, to create heal and restore, our truth our purpose our blessing, to deny love is the fabric of consciousness, is to deny the truth of creation and spirit.

Stephen Rowlands

EVERYONE SPEAKS OF BEING

IN THE MOMENT

YOU ARE THE MOMENT

DEVELOP PEACE WITHIN

© Stephen Rowlands

EVERY NEW DAY IS A OPPORTUNITY
LIVE LOVE AND LEARN

CREATE

Stephen Rowlands

Alive

The genesis of creation
Gave life to all things known and unknown
I am alive so I am creation
Universal and eternal
I am ready to put creation to the test
What is real life
Anything I want life to be
Surely the creation of creation
Is truth

Stephen Rowlands

Spiritual Development Is An Opening Of The Heart

To Discover The Hidden Truths Of The Heart

Love Is The Power Of The Universe
To Live Your Truth With Love
Is The Most Powerful Expression Of Life

Inspiration from Spirit Guide Running Bear 08/11/19

Mother Moon

I gaze upon you benevolent mother moon

Stormy clouds do not disturb your warmth

I share with you the colours of my heart

Knowing someone somewhere is gazing upon you

This night is powerful and magical

Connecting me to someone somewhere

Mother moon you are the collector

Of wishes and dreams your vision

Connects us all in heart and mind

Stephen Rowlands

Just A Dream

Perhaps my life so far has been just a dream

My dream ebbs away into yesterday

As I become conscious of the new day

A heart without hurt a mind without torment a soul without regret

Is surely a miraculous thing

As the morning sun heralds in a new day

As I awaken to this new dawn serene in heart and mind

What about my lady is she just a dream

My heart fills with loving warmth as I contemplate the dream

My heart knowing she is my love today and every day

My thoughts conspire a new invention

To live life as a lucid dream for the future is

The undiscovered country for me to explore

And create with calm mind and good heart

No longer just a dream but a garden of creation

As Eden once fabled was the apple bitten the snake defied

I can now journey on my path with love as my guide

Stephen Rowlands

The Voice Of My Heart

Silence manifests a stillness in early morn
Calling my heart to rise to it's highest self
From my material being inertia in thought
Struggling against the shackles of my daily life
Twisting my emotions to anger denying love
Awoken and alive the selfless love of spirit
Envelopes the radiant light of love within me
Beckoning me to a pathway of service
My truth my way my light
May never this worldly darkness fade

Stephen Rowlands

Your New Day

Your day is a new page in your life

Before your feet hit the floor

You have the power to

Choose acceptance over dread

Understanding over confusion

Calm over anger

Creation over inertia

Opportunity over defeat

Looking forward over regret

Happiness over sadness

Love of life over bitterness

Your new day is your creation

Life is a state of mind

Positive balances negative in this life

Have a good day

Stephen Rowlands

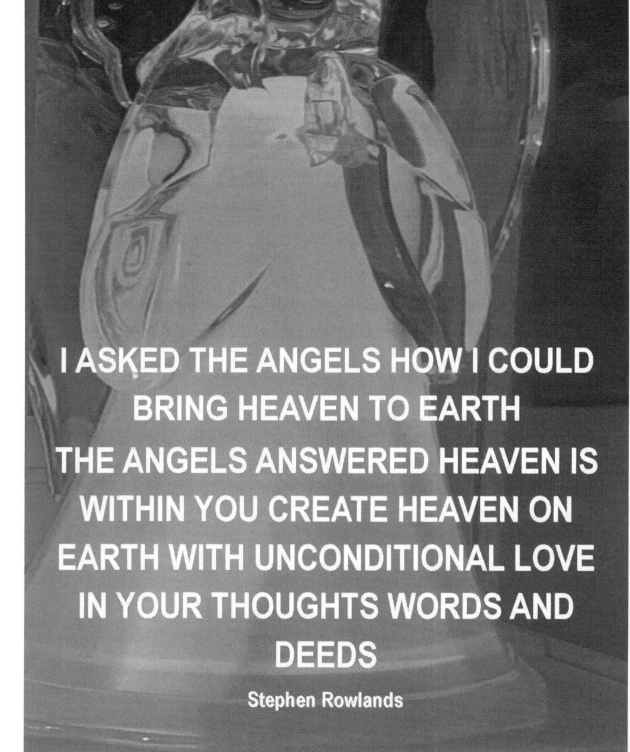

I ASKED THE ANGELS HOW I COULD BRING HEAVEN TO EARTH THE ANGELS ANSWERED HEAVEN IS WITHIN YOU CREATE HEAVEN ON EARTH WITH UNCONDITIONAL LOVE IN YOUR THOUGHTS WORDS AND DEEDS

Stephen Rowlands

Stop The World

Stop the world my beloved has died

I want the world to take time to mourn

Abandoned in this moment

As the new day marches on in time

I stand here in solitary sorrow

Physical death is final and unforgiving

I will never see you again in this life

Stop the world give me time

My beloved's presence is no more

Just memories of once was

To keep my beloved alive in heart and mind

I wish to tell you of my beloved

The blessing he was to me and family

Stop the world and listen

My beloved has died

Stephen Rowlands 22/12/19

Beginning

I seek you neath the half moon

My spirit fades without your gentle feeling

Eternity in afterlife will judge our purpose

The sun will rise and I will leave

My love for you neath the half moon

Looking up to the morning blue

Your presence is gone

Thankful for the sacred gift of life

My purpose becomes clear

Now I can seek out my life and truth

Without the illusion of your love

Inner creation is mine to command

The future beckons me to become

Stephen Rowlands

Above The Rain Clouds

Walking above the rain clouds my mind elevated to blue sky and sun

The rain falls as past sorrows above all my sorrows I now see

The vanity of love selfish illusions of a soul to love

Wanting someone to love blinded my minds eye to love

All I needed to do was be and grow in heart and mind

The search was not to find love but to be love

Enriching my soul and life walking above the rain clouds

Abundance of love in heart and mind my love for you

Fills me in a wave of euphoria cleansing all perception

Of future life with you we are to be and become

Two souls entwined within the destiny of love

Stephen Rowlands

At Peace

I welcome my old friend silence
To calm the noise of my mind
A welcome visitor to give me respite
From all that troubles me
Ego bows to humility in silence
Awakening the sentience of heart
Compassion for my persecutor
Is my lesson
Healing and calming my mental storm
Silence bids me to become silent
Within this moment of clarity
All that matters is silence
As in all moments
Peace is a natural state of being
Stephen Rowlands

Hearts Awakening

The blood red of the rose has filled my eyes with lustful passion

It's thorns have stabbed deep into my heart oh what an enigma love is

I have flown to the sun my heart soaring like an eagle

On loves celestial wings and been cast into the deepest darkest abyss

When love had abandoned me solitude was my healer

As I navigated the turbulent waters of self discovery

Seeking the truth of my heart love is the truth within my heart

A selfless love to be given unconditionally to all who seek spirit

A woman to love my heart was an illusion to me

My heart slept in loves sweet hibernation I now awaken

To a lady with the beautiful truth of love within her heart

She now takes my hand and walks beside me

With all her love and sorrow deep within her knowing eyes

I kiss her deeply as we blend our awakening hearts

Stephen Rowlands

Trouble And Strife

I love my life
No trouble and strife
I love my wife
Guided through my heart
Abundance of love
Blessings from heaven
Flowing through my days
Trouble and strife
No more
Love and purpose in spirit
My life has begun
Stephen Rowlands

ALL THAT I AM

In gentle slumber my heart opens to all that is unseen
Through the long sigh of the night my soul beckons me
All is possible All is infinite from the small room of my perception
I dream all that I can become is here as candlelight flickers
Darkness shrouds the flame my grief manifests here
Oh permanent light tell me the flame never dies

© Stephen Rowlands

Weary

Weary of the wheel of material life, expending energy draining going nowhere fast in rotation, tired and forlorn must power the greed engine, sitting with my wine asking the question why am I programmed to work this wheel, is it the knowledge of age that speaks, or my creaking body, that will not allow me to do what I once did, I am weary of the systemic ideal, that wants me in my place, I have worked my whole life, feeding energy to the greed engine, the life love and laughter, I have missed whilst working this dam wheel, is the tax that I have paid, for a comfortable life.

When I am exhausted and can no longer feed the greed engine, I will be discarded and replaced, worn out for what purpose I ask, the best years passed by, hindsight is a beautiful future lived in the past, a day dream that I can no longer regret, I should have stepped off the wheel, when my dreams could have been loved and lived, weary of futile work serving the corperate machine, that nourishes the few but wastes the many.

I have had too many years of doing big favours, for the businesses I have served, I have gained nothing from doing favours, I have lost time to live breathe and love, you call again asking for a big favour, this time I cannot oblige, because time is limited for me and priceless, I will waste no more of my precious time, making you rich and me weary.

Stephen Rowlands

Be Still

Be still as the candle flame

Within the peace of the moment

Gain strength in your truth

Your world may change

But the truth of your eternal spirit

Will never change be still

As the storms of life pass over you

And the sun rises again

Inspired by Jerome Franciscan Monk Spirit Guide

Stephen Rowlands

Pictures On My Wall

Returning home weary, after a long week at work, negative emotion gnawing at my guts, anger turbulent within my mind, like the most violent lightening storm. I remind myself I am at home now, and that I am so blessed to have a home, on this cold wet and windy night.

My flat warm and cosy as can be, I change into my comfies, so good to be home, away from the corperate ego driven bullshit, that pays my bills, my home is my sanctuary, where I can breathe and be me.

Lying on my bed, candlelight illuminating the colours of my flat, looking at the pictures on my wall, telling the story of my past and present, a feeling of amazement washes over me. pictorial memories of holidays family and friends, my spiritual pathway, looking at me from my wall.

The summer day of my higher self, now calming my storm, reminding me it is not good to dwell, in self created negative of ego, the mind should always seek, the truth in heart, now I am glad I took the pictures on my wall, showing me where I have been, and where to go with blessings, thank you pictures on my wall.

Stephen Rowlands

Little Acts

Little acts of kindness are gifts from the heart
To friend's and foes patience is our guide
No matter the hurt and pain we give and receive
Little acts of kindness will be our epitaph
To report how we lived and loved
Our anger will not be remembered
By those who's feelings we hurt
Our little acts of kindness will live
Within the hearts and mind's
Of friends and foes for evermore
Stephen Rowlands

Dedicated To
June Moore
President
Walton On Thames Spiritual Church

Angel

Finding solace in peace and quiet away from burden and noise

I sit still as the candle flame my heart open in service

Colours of love light shining outward from my heart

Love fills my awareness spirit are present my senses awaken

A connection of love and unity a bond

Between two worlds present and eternal

Within my minds eye I see an angel

Serene in blue and white light

She comes to me face to face within her beautiful eyes

A wisdom of time and space universal mind and creation

My limited earthly mind cannot comprehend

The angel opens my awareness to universal mind

Connecting me to all who wish to speak in loves service

Giving the teachings of universal love and life

Stephen Rowlands

Far Away

Death is a truth of life everyone dies
The hardest fact of life is that life goes on
Our hearts in sorrow never seem to heal
Whether our beloved abandon us or pass away
Life moves forward in a constant rhythm
It is very easy for friends to say
Your beloved is in a better place
Let go just move forward live your life
Our grief deep within stands us still
Heart and mind craving the presence
Of our beloved far away
Life is a journey in this world and beyond
We must weep for our loved ones passed away
And bid a fond farewell with love
To our beloved who journey far away
Love has no boundaries in time and space
For love is eternal and cannot pass away
Let us give our love and blessing safe journey
To our beloved who journey far away

Stephen Rowlands

Coloured Paper And Shiny Buttons

White line high up in the sky, oh how I wish I could fly, my eyes the world to see, heart free as air to embrace, in awe of this wonder of creation. Feet firmly planted on mother earth, my minds eye gazing on the blue orb where I reside, in infinite space I am aware I exist in an existence shackled by human consciousness, where there is always a price to pay.

We place value on everything, but no value on life, enslaved to the devils of money and status, makes demons of us all, as we do what we can to get, a pocketful of the coloured paper and shiny buttons we need. Survival or success are the two divisions in life, the have nots and the haves,are divided by greed, it is only those who succeed, can afford their mouths to feed.

Coloured paper and shiny buttons have dominion over our world, we the willing servants, bowing to the rule of coloured paper and shiny buttons, our masters placed over us. The banks we fill to bulging, spew out coloured paper from holes in the wall, people go hungry and starve, for lack of coloured paper and shiny buttons, no medical treatment, illness, suffering, and death. for those without a pocketful of coloured paper shiny buttons, we kill and steal all to gain more coloured paper and shiny buttons.

We the human race value and live in material ignorance, we need to embrace a simple truth, money is just coloured paper and shiny buttons, all of creation has been given to us free of charge, we must live free together, the value of life is Love, Kindness, Compassion, Tolerance, and Peace for all, we must care for the source of life Mother Earth, who we pollute and destroy all for coloured paper and shiny buttons, one day the human race will be destroyed, for the love and greed of coloured paper and shiny buttons.

Stephen Rowlands

Soul Perception

We judge others in our earthbound mental bondage

Be aware in mind the soul does not judge anyone

All emotion thought and deed expressed

Here on earth is for our souls growth

Countless physical existences we as souls have lived

First to understand we must become to begin

The journey to pure love and divine being

Judgement is the ignorance of the fool

Be aware every soul here on earth is on a path

To be cleansed of dark human consciousness

Becoming pure divine light for all eternity

Stephen Rowlands

Love Is Deeper Now

My journey of life has taken me down the roads, of solitude, loneliness, failure, anger, pain, love, service and triumph, the pathway of change brought me to you love is deeper now.

Your love brings a peace to my soul, that my mind cannot invent, my heart reaches out for your love seeking unity with your soul, love is deeper now.

The light of your love creates a rainbow, through the rain encouraging me to be the best I can be, love is deeper now.

My love for you ascends to the stars above, every day I give thanks for you, love is deeper now.

The gift of your love gives me balance between earth and sky, I will never be alone, love is deeper now.

We choose to walk together in heart and mind on this journey of life, love is deeper now.

Today we blend our hearts together within the sanctuary of marriage, loves lessons learned love is deeper now.

Stephen Rowlands

60 Years

I am an expression of a love far greater than myself and human existence

My spirit expressed by love to this life here in physical form to experience

All emotion human existence has to offer a physical material trial

By fire for the soul cleansing away my darkness for the eternal journey

To become a love I cannot imagine in limited material mind

Open all encompassing unconditional my awakening of spiritual awareness

Becoming as one with a love far greater than myself

60 physical years my consciousness has existed here on the earth plane

Seeking the truth questioning my being asking where do I belong

Self illusion faded away by a need to be truly myself the answer became clear

As I opened my heart to the truth of a love far greater than myself within

May my open heart never close to divine love eternal serene and still

Stephen Rowlands

Floating In Purple

Meditation is my escape from the illusion of mortal emotion

Floating in purple my preferred state of mind

Healing my mind and body in balance with my soul

The eternal radiance of compassion liberating me

From ego and doubt my heart set free to love

Within this universal consciousness of unconditional love

Floating in purple the serenity of eternity permeates my truth

Connected in being to the mind of creation within this eternal moment

Human desire and frailty in heart and mind disappear

I am invisible and complete as one with divine eternity

Stephen Rowlands

Locked Away

Locked away by covid19 stir crazy these four walls are closing in

Must get out and walk get some air I am locked away but no longer

Running the rat race I am free to think and feel life passing by no more

I have time to appreciate being alive blessed not to be sick

Free to walk and talk thanking passers by for keeping social distance

We need to connect be in touch connecting with mother nature

How beautiful she is blinded by the race to the vibrant beauty

Of mother nature all around me living and breathing as I am

Locked away I am learning more to life than being a runner in the race

Locked away I open my heart to a loving connection to all life

This world is a stage may I no longer be a rat in the race

This life in all it's tragedy and blessings may I play my part

Express my life art living life happy and free

Stephen Rowlands

HeartSpace

Awakening my mind to a new awareness evolving within

Harmful emotions being washed away

Ego is a comfortable room to dwell on the faults of others

My mind focuses on the pathway ahead

Freeing me of spiteful ego fading out all distractions

From my purpose to serve creating a powerful heart space

New and open to be filled with love and spirit

Who am I to judge how another walks this path

When I like them are called to serve

All that matters is how I walk my path of service

Stephen Rowlands

EVERY HEART

EVERY HEART KNOWS THE WISDOM OF LOVE

EVERY HEART OPENS IN HUMILTY

EVERY HEART CAN SERVE AND BE KIND

EVERY HEART SHINES IN COMPASSION

EVERY HEART SERENE IN PEACE

EVERY HEART CAN FEEL AFRAID

EVERY HEART CAN SING A SONG OF WOE

EVERY HEART CAN FEEL ALONE

EVERY HEART FINDS STRENGTH IN FAITH

EVERY HEART SWAYS IN INDECISION

EVERY HEART SHOULD SPEAK IT'S TRUTH

EVERY HEART CAN BE CONFUSED

ALL MY HEARTS I GIVE TO YOU

FOR MY LOVE IN HONOUR TRUE

STEPHEN ROWLANDS

Willow Tree

Silently in majestic beauty you stand amidst

Our intrusion your beautiful truth for all to see

Mother earth energy circulating through you

Reaching out to the sky back to earth

Enfolding me in a loving warmth

Sunshine through your leaves

The wind blows you speak to me

Of the harmonious balance in all things

Everything is as it is meant to be

The emotional kaleidoscope of mind

Disturbs the harmony of life

We must be still to appreciate the balance of life

Accepting the storms come and go

Swaying with the breeze embracing the flow

Of energy all around us all the time

Your peaceful serenity is my teacher

Teaching me peace of mind wise old willow tree

Stephen Rowlands

Homesick Heart

The journey of the heart is seeking out a place

Where the heart can call home if such a place exists

In this myriad of possibilities expectations always fall short

Of what truly manifests in the meditation of life

Memories reflect back like the broken shards of a mirror

Strewn on the floor of the mind the homesick heart knows

There is no way back for the heart is the wanderer

The loner bound in time journeying towards the inevitable fate

As all fades away in our world of matter and time

Within our mortal existence we accept change as we grow old

Because we are mortal it is all we can perceive

But the heart is the inner child timeless and eternal

Time is of no importance to the homesick heart

Only to be where the heart belongs

Stephen Rowlands

Opening My Heart To Blessings

I did not want to give away the film's we loved to watch

As I gave my friend your favourite films

I felt a release of my memories watching westerns with you

I realised I was letting you go but I know it is our next step

I know my friend will enjoy watching them

Bringing me a loving inner warmth in memory of you

It is a new day the sun is shining a spring chill in the air

Feeling like a boy new day new adventure

My heart open to what the day will bring

Walking to escape from my comfy inertia

Cleaning out my mental junk nature surrounds me

Blessing my eyes with her vibrant beauty blessing my soul

To be alive here and now in this quiet abundance

Of my life and love my wedding ring a sacred symbol

That I belong to one heart I am finally home

Blessed that spirit inspire me with words

That bring comfort and kindness to people in need

I am thankful to spirit for opening my heart

This past 5 years a journey of grief and loneliness

To finding my home my love my life

Stephen Rowlands

Humility Opens Our Heart To Everything

Stephen Rowlands

My Friend

You walk with me side by side

Through my storms and summer days

You help me focus when I doubt myself

Encourage me when I am anxious

Comfort me when love and friendship are no more

You are the light in my darkness

The voice of my soul guiding me in truth

When I am lost my choices taking me away

From the path of purpose and enlightenment

You love me no matter how much I have forsaken you

Arms open wide welcoming me back to love

Thank you my friend for this life in eternity

For all my lessons and blessings

My one true eternal friend

Stephen Rowlands

Colour Of My Love

Within all the passion and emotion of this world

Pink is the colour of my infinite love for you

Love is a spectrum of many celestial colours

But none a more vibrant hue than my love for you

Your angelic love is the healer of my heart

The gentleness of your spirit opened my eyes to love

You want nor expect nothing from me but my love

Allowing me the freedom to love you without condition

My life has been a long exploration for love

I have discovered my love for you is pink

Stephen Rowlands

Love You

My spirit weeps for you in your sadness

Love cannot replace the love you have lost

All I can do is love you

Till the dark clouds of grief float away

And the sun shines within your heart

Holding you close in my love

The healing balm of my love will comfort you

Death is as certain as life

Grief is the sorrow of love far away

Time is our unkind master as life ticks away

Your heart must say farewell to your beloved

I will love you till the sun shines again

Stephen Rowlands

Just Our Imagination

Imagining you imagining me

In who's mind do we belong

Yours or mine what is this consciousness

That joins us in this reality of time and space

I am here you are there alive unseen

Your thoughtful energy creating the moon and stars

And all that I see and know we speak everyday

How can we be as one is it my imagination

Or is it your thoughts that give you a voice

I can perceive within my minds eye

And my thoughts you can see in your imagination

Speaking in thoughts to one another

Together alive within the reality of our imagination

Stephen Rowlands

Universal Mind

All life is the creation of the mind of God

Manifesting in the form of matter

Universal mind the life giving truth

Of our being and purpose to be alive

To evolve and grow in God's plan for us

Why do we ignore the mind of God

Speaking to us of universal life and love

We dwell in the darkness of the mortal mind

Let us open our minds to the mind of God within

Embracing the knowledge of eternal life and truth

We cannot imagine within the illusion of mortality

There is no death all life is eternal in consciousness

Live this truth in your temporary mortal existence

Your life will become your truth in all eternity

Inspired By Jerome Franciscan Monk Spirit Guide

Stephen Rowlands

Spiritualist

I am a spiritualist I do not believe in death

I know life is eternal I am alive in consciousness

Why do you believe death is the end of life

And not know the truth all life is eternal

There are no ends only beginnings for our true selves

The eternal spirit to rise from the mortal body to begin again

Conscious and alive within the realms of spirit

Spirit teachers guide me on this earth plane

Helping me to cope in mind through my trials

Teaching me love is the essence of my eternal being

Humility is my strength

Compassion is my empathy with all life

Kindness is the power of love

To express the great spirit selflessly in service

My purpose and truth in earth life

Stephen Rowlands

Do not compare your progress to others
Your journey is yours to walk
Focus on your own talent and growth

Stephen Rowlands

Yesterday

Yesterday was my journey to today

What did I do yesterday that got me here today

Footsteps in time is all that life appears to be

Today will be yesterday when tomorrow dawns

My thoughts and actions yesterday have created my today

Yesterday I rested from night's toil until my mind became clear

Today my heart and mind free in spirit to live and love

Expressing my truth for all around me to perceive

My universal life's worth is my state of heart and mind

My journey in this body is life to death

Knowing this day will become my tomorrow

May my words and deeds today be for the greater good

So that tomorrow I am at peace with myself

And life is at peace with me

Stephen Rowlands

My Cross

Ancient symbol and message of holy sacrifice

And freedom to eternal life he had to die

For us to see the way to the truth and light

To forgive us all of our sins I can forgive

I have sinned I am no angel

My cross is my reminder of the light

Of who I truly am when I opened my eye to spirit

My cross a gift from spirit and my guide Berenice

Gold wisdom and divine service

Silver mediumship to be the messenger of spirit

The cross the symbol of the man who died for me

To live my truth of spiritual service

My cross symbol of my purpose and destiny

Stephen Rowlands

Freewill

Everyone moans about how life is treating them

Have we ever asked ourselves

How are we treating life

All things change as we make our choices

Accept change as we have invoked our freewill

We can develop our freewill through the lessons of change

Or we can decay by not accepting

The freewill flow of change with all it's challenges

We have our freewill choices to make

Then change knocks on the door

Not accepting our freewill creates change will lead to our downfall

In a spiral of regret anger and bitterness

We must accept that change is as certain

As ageing and death but life goes on

Seek to create our lives for the greater good

Invoke our freewill with love and purpose

No matter what change destroys

We will find better days will come

Growing with gratitude in spirit and heart

Stephen Rowlands

A Day To Live

Morning light awakens me from my slumber

I lie here within this comforting solitude

Warm and content in my dreams philosophies

Envisioning what I need to do today

Living life as a automaton is not living at all

In this laborious work rest work cycle

What do I need to do to feel alive today

I must make today count to awaken my heart

To leave my hearts passion for life on this day

An imprint in time for me to fondly remember

I give thanks for the new day and ask

What trials has the new day to challenge me

This day is a divine gift for my spirit to shine

Whatever I do today is a statement about myself

I must make the day count to live and feel alive

Look up to the sky take a breath of fresh air

In awe of this beautiful creation all around me

Love laughter kindness and compassion are my gifts to share

Expressing my life art through my heart

Making this day count as a day I have lived

Stephen Rowlands

Zion

I explore my inner self seeking a state of Zion
I know the inner state of Zion exists
As the masters love and serve humanity there
Love is my only guide who I must trust
On this perilous journey to a spiritual utopia
Through my doubts fears and illusions
Love will guide calming my insecurities
Making sense of all my emotions
I must be true to love to raise my consciousness
To heightened levels of awareness and being
Many believe Zion does not exist
Like Atlantis lost long ago in legend
Existing in human consciousness
Man believes heaven within is unreachable
I trust my heart to know It's home is in Zion

Stephen Rowlands

Beating Heart

Division blinds the clear vision of year 2020

Sins never forgiven past lessons never learned

Ignorance consumes the human race

Let us open our minds and know everyone has a beating heart

Come together brothers and sisters of earth

Love is our forgotten guide to equality

Peace for all must now be our united mission

Seek to love one another from the soul of unity

No matter the colour of the skin everyone has a beating heart

The human race needs to awaken to the simple truth

All life is the miracle of creation we must not deny the miracle

Hatred of a peoples colour is mankind's wicked lie to control

everyone has a beating heart

Stephen Rowlands

Dreamer

What purpose is in my dreams

Should I just discard my dreams

As the futile pursuit of a man seeking destiny

Or employ them to guide my footsteps

Into the barren future navigating a course

Towards my fate and purpose in this chosen reality

There is one who senses my dreams and believes in me

Alive and conscious within each other

We sow and reap on a journey that has no end

Stephen Rowlands

I Am Alive
I Am Eternal
I Am Conscious
I Am Energy
I Am Light
I Am Colour
I Am Love
I Am Truth
I Am Spirit
I Am Soul

Stephen Rowlands

Conscious

I wish I had a force field around my heart
To spare my mind from the dagger of your ego
Judgement is ignorant when pride has motive
How dare you judge me and deny my service
I have feelings and they are hurt
Awakening my sleeping anger a tempest rises within
Torturing my developed state of inner peace
My teaching tells me to calm the storm
Revenge will only bury me alongside you
A bitter lesson now sweet in the learning
My truth is to serve spirit whenever I am called
Guided by spirit I must not ask to serve
Today my awakened higher self speaks it's reason
To focus my heart on my God given gift of creation
Silencing my raging anger peace comforts my disturbed soul
I welcome in the new day full of hope
Conscious I can manifest the peaceful serenity of love
Through my thoughts words and deeds
For the upliftment of myself and all

Stephen Rowlands

Everyday

The light of spirit that shines brightly within you

Is your loving gift to the world

Never allow your light be dimmed

By the ignorance of others who deny your worth

Your brilliant light fades with self doubt

Ego is the light of the fool only the fool can see

Develop the gifts of the spirit within

To become aware in a peaceful serenity

Let not the perception of others deter you

From your chosen path shine your light

For all to see share your loving gift

With all who seek your light

Your peers opinions of you are no measure

Of your worth in Gods purpose for you

Everyday know you are gifted in Gods plan

God knows you are worthy of the path

Everyday focus on your journey

Be true to the light of spirit within

Stephen Rowlands

Colours

Spirit light vibrant and serene
Colour my consciousness with peace
Stillness is the perfection of spirit
A state of mind I seek to attain
The colours of my emotions in constant flux
I need to be still for spirit light
To radiate through my being
The colours of my love to rise
Permeating all realities of consciousness
To be one with myself and spirit light
My negative emotions and discord now sleep
Giving me the freedom to breathe
To be alive in my universal truth
Living on this mortal earth plane
Is a cross to bear for we who walk it's path
Spirit light brings peace to my trials
Opening my heart to all possibilities

Stephen Rowlands

Fire And Grace

Unknown creation beckons a new age

Have I the fire and grace to serve

As I gaze upon time passed by

Spirit have walked beside me

Patiently waiting for me to cast out my illusions

Spirit love illuminates my darkness

As I look up to the light

From the depths of my regret

Once a young man full of fire and grace

The path of my illusions seeking

What I am not love is blind

Merlin looks at me with a loving warmth

All realities perceived have been my souls learning

Destiny is now I must act

Through the truth of my hearts journey

Serving spirit with fire and grace

Stephen Rowlands

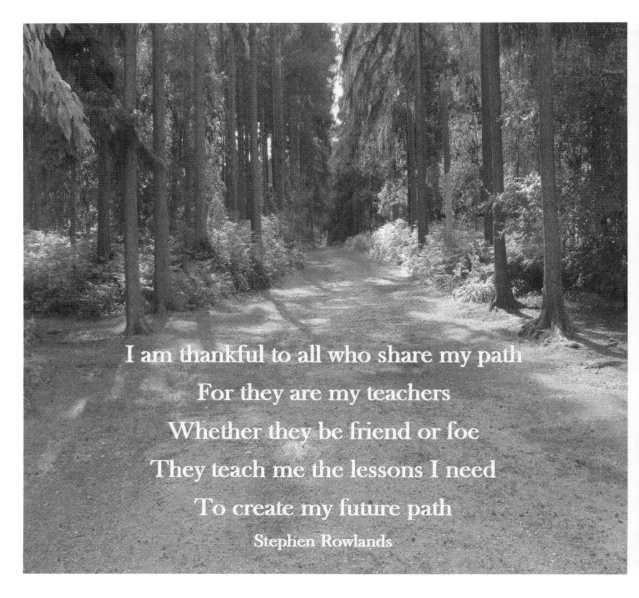

I am thankful to all who share my path

For they are my teachers

Whether they be friend or foe

They teach me the lessons I need

To create my future path

Stephen Rowlands

Thankyou For Reading

Stephen Rowlands

Printed in Great Britain
by Amazon

85225980R00070